Angels Walking With Us

True Stories of Faith, Hope and Miracles

George Popovici

PUBLISHER'S INFORMATION

First Edition.

Stories told by Rosemary Barboza, Lee Cowden, MD, Vernon Dawson, Jennifer Dionne, Beverly, Pastor Jordan Jacobson, John Kohler, Chelsea Leander, James Russo, David Simpson, Jill Stevenson and Ron Zagarri are reprinted with permission.

The EBook Bakery

ISBN 978-1-938517-20-4

© 2013 by George Popovici

Author contact: www.angelswalkingwithus.net

ACKNOWLEDGMENTS

I would like to express my gratitude to the many people who saw me through this book; to all those who provided support, particularly those who shared their personal testimonies.

To my friend and mentor, Maureen Hancock, who said I would write and publish a book that would help many who need encouragement, especially in times of trouble and despair.

The following people that never stopped believing in me: Josephine Almeida, all Babu relatives, Rose and John Barboza, Christopher Blake, Hazel Britto, Deputy Chief Bob Brown, Forrest Carr, John Carvalho, YW Chow, Penni Conner, Dr. Lee Cowden, Rose Dalton, Vernon Dawson, Jennifer Dionne, Kimberly Doheny, Paul Dubois, Michael Durand, John Fallon, Becky Favors, Dana Fennelly, Liz Ferreira, Nicholas Gianturco, Mark Gunsalus, Craig Hallstrom, Michael Hayhurst, Dr. Richard Horowitz, Carla Housh, Terry and Margie Howser, Jordan S.C. Jacobson, Sr., Lisa Johnson, Chief Bill Karalis, Dr. Amiram Katz, Chuck Kelly, Rhode Island Attorney General Peter Kilmartin, John Kohler, Dr. Georg Kroiss, Barbara Laird, Karen Lea, Kelley Lennon, Karen Mac-Beth, Richard and Shirley Marcin, Thomas May, Kevin and Dena McLaughlin, Wanda Beth McManus, Don Michaud, Julie Moore, Alan and Andrea Nichelson, Col. Steven O'Donnell RISP, Tom Patton, Bernard Peloquin, Philip Platow, Jeff Popham, Richard and Flora Popovici, Kristen Richter, Tom and Shirley Rodrigues, Jim and Sandie Russo, Werner Schweiger, Tim and Stacy Schultz,, David Simpson, Jeff Smith, Michael and Lisa Smith, Andy Soutter, Ruth Souza, Ken Stann, Jill Stevenson, Dr. Marc Theroux, Joseph Walsh, Donna Warren, Gail Whittenburger, Ron Zagarri, Domnica Ziu, Steven Ziu and Israel Zorola.

To my editor, author, Katherine Mayfield, and to publishing consultant Michael Grossman who took the extra time and effort. My book coach, Lisa Tener.

DEDICATION

I dedicate this book to my ancestors who paved the path
and to my children who are my legacy.

Popovici

TABLE OF CONTENTS

GEORGE POPOVICI'S MEDICAL LOG

Since October 2005 to date:

$246,000.00 spent "out of pocket" for office visits, specialty laboratory tests, treatments, supplements and travel

48,000 Miles traveled for office visits and specialized treatment in the USA and abroad

364 Vials of oral medications (Liquid and pill form)

212 Office Visits

42 Physicians seen

33 Sets of Laboratory Tests

29 Intramuscular injections

11 Emergency Room Visits

7 Hospital Admittances (Two-five days duration or longer)

6 MRI of the brain and spine

5 Blood Ozone Treatments

4 Hearing Tests

4 Vision Tests including an ERG as Massachusetts Eye and Ear Hospital

3 Spinal Taps

3 Peripherally Inserted Catheters (PIC Lines)

3 Colonoscopies

2 Nerve biopsies (Punch skin from you ankle or thigh)

2 Dark field Microscopy of my blood

2 Sleep studies

1 case of nearly fatal sepsis (blood infection)

1 Pulmonary Embolism (blood clot in lung)

PREFACE

God and his angels are always around us, protecting us and sending messages. We often become too busy and involved with our day to day lives to see the true meaning of why we are here and what our mission and purpose is on earth. We ignore the signs and signals that are very much present in daily life, and which, when we are open to receive them, continually reassure us of these simple truths:

1. **There is a God.**

2. **Everything happens for a reason.**

3. **Never lose hope.**

4. **With hope, miracles happen.**

I was one of those people who was too wrapped up in my own agenda to be aware of any kind of deeper meaning in my life. Although I went through the motions of being good and helpful—I served others as an altar boy, Eagle Scout, Emergency Medical Technician, Volunteer Firefighter, coach, community volunteer, and Safety Engineer—I was completely unable to deeply connect with people on a higher level, or to see what lies beyond the physical world as we know it.

All that changed when my life hit the bottom. I became deathly, and mysteriously ill.

In the past nine years, I have traveled the entire nation seeking medical attention, hoping to find a cure for an illness that ravaged my body. I became obsessed with finding an answer so I could stop the decline and restore my health. I jumped from one world-class medical center to the next in numerous states, and saw 42 physicians in all. I even sought out a world-famous doctor who had a reputation similar to "House" from the popular television series, to review and consult with me.

Before this illness struck, I was 46 years old, and had it all: great health, an accomplished family, three outstanding children, successful parents and siblings, a gorgeous home, rock-solid finances, fantastic career, and good, close friends. One might say I was a perfect example of success as we often define it in today's industrialized society.

In the autumn of 2005, I suddenly became very ill. By the spring of 2006, my blood was clotting, and I had developed a pulmonary embolism in my left lung. Doctors suggested that I should have a medical proxy appointed and standing by. The picture was grim.

I have experienced seven hospitalizations, scores of tests and procedures at the finest medical centers in the nation, and spent nearly $250,000 of my own money to become well. I continue with symptoms that include the loss of my eyesight, hearing, and my senses of touch, taste, and smell as a result of continuing nervous system damage caused by advanced neurological Lyme disease, an elusive killer disease that affects hundreds of thousands of people all over the globe.

I was totally unprepared to have my life completely flipped upside down, but the experience has given me the gift of understanding who I truly am and what my mission is. My mission, and knowing that I am *never* alone in it, has been the key to my survival.

Nine years later I am still here. So a word of advice, if anyone tells you that there is no hope, that you should accept your situation, or if they laugh at you, get up and walk away. Never give up, and NEVER stop believing.

This book is about believing, about faith, hope, and love. It is best summed up in this Bible verse: **"Walk by faith and not by sight." 2 Corinthians 5:7**

My story is true, as are the powerful, amazing stories that follow mine, told to me by real people. The renowned Maureen Hancock (the world-famous psychic and medium) met with me not once, not twice, but three times to encourage me to share these messages of love and inspiration with those in need of the hope.

There is no question in my mind that I was led to this belief when I was at the lowest, most desperate and hopeless point of my life. I had to see who I really am, beneath the persona, so that I can focus on my true purpose here on earth.

It still amazes me how many people, young and old, wealthy and poor, ill and well, cannot see beyond the physical world we live in. Some have little or no faith in anything except what they can touch and see. To that point, this is NOT a book about world religion or a "how-to" for those who want to practice the mechanics of the same. I learned long ago that man-made rules cannot bring you to your highest levels of enlightenment.

This is a book about faith and belief: that the key to "knowing" truly begins with being still, listening, and focusing on God and his angels.

First, I will share my own journey with you, so you can see how faith and belief can completely transform a life filled with sadness, illness, and pain into something worthwhile: a life with purpose. Then, in section two, others tell their stories...inspiring stories of divine faith that paved a path with life-saving miracles.

Maureen told me that people would come to me to share in what I have learned. And come they have, sometimes in the most unassuming settings. My wish is that the stories I share will offer hope and faith to those who focus only on the "here and now" but don't consider the larger picture.

PROLOGUE

Maureen Hancock,
Lifeline to Hope and Purpose

*Reputation is what men and women think of us;
character is what God and Angels know of us"*
Thomas Paine

When I first learned of Maureen Hancock in 2009, I had been chronically ill for nearly 3½ years. After spiraling downward from a life which had seemed perfect in every way, I had become hopeless about the possibility of my healing, and I was very sad. I had spent over $100,000 in non-covered medical expenses at that point in time, consulted with top doctors at the best medical facilities in the nation, and was still searching for answers to the strange, debilitating disease that was robbing my energy, eyesight, and senses of taste, touch, and smell. It was not uncommon for me to sit and cry for an hour or two as I reflected on my utter disbelief about what was happening to me. There were no answers, and very sporadic suggestions for treatment. It wasn't until later that I learned I had a rare form of chronic Lyme disease.

When I was ill, I felt that God was not listening to me, and I believed that I was being punished for the wrongdoings I might have committed here on earth. I was on a collision course with death—all of my efforts to regain my health yielded little result. My world was dark and filled with hopelessness, and I spent a fair amount of time in sadness, focusing on dark thoughts. I was just existing, with no thoughts of hope or love, and my health was declining very rapidly.

Sad, perplexed, and seemingly broken, I tried to continue with some normal regimen of life. I reported to work as I did every day, and one day as I walked the halls of my office complex, I bumped into two ladies whom I had assisted years before with ergonomic adjustments on the job. As part of my training and duties as a safety engineer, I am responsible for ensuring that employees are properly seated and positioned at their work

4

stations, to minimize lost time from back pain injuries. I took a liking to these kind, warm-hearted women. They were no-nonsense people who say what is on their mind and would be willing to give a hug to someone in need.

As I moved toward them, they noticed me with my head down and looking sad. One of them, named Liz, looked directly into my eyes, and asked me how I was doing. Soon the conversation centered on my health and my struggles. Seeing that I was completely out of sorts, Liz suggested that I see Maureen Hancock.

I distinctly recall saying, "Maureen who?"

She replied, "Maureen Hancock...she is amazing." Liz started beaming when she spoke about Maureen and the gifts she has that allow people to believe there is hope, and specifically, that God has a plan for everyone. "You see, Maureen can communicate with those who have passed away to let the surviving loved ones here on earth know that they are okay," Liz said. I was silent and moved as Liz explained in detail some of the people who were completely converted from sadness and hopelessness to vibrancy with Maureen's help.

Liz had no idea how desperate I was to have confidence that I would be okay, either here on earth or somewhere beyond with God. Although I had always had belief and faith, I had been questioning all of it, especially why I had become so ill. Everything in my world was crumbling: my marriage, my career, and my health. I didn't understand why.

Liz urged me to visit Maureen's website and obtain tickets to see her. Liz indicated that there was a three-year waiting list to see her privately, and even at that there were no guarantees. I thanked Liz for the information, and pondered it for a day. Me being me, I thought I would make an attempt to see Maureen directly; after all, I was quite ill and desperate for answers. So I called her office and spoke with a very kind lady named Wanda Beth McManus, who was Maureen's assistant at the time. I explained my situation to Wanda. She was very polite, and reiterated what Liz had told me a day earlier—that I would probably not be able to see Maureen privately for a few years, but that she would check with Maureen. She asked me to call her the following day.

Waiting another day seems like an eternity when your world is dark and you have no hope and feel worthless. Somehow I got through it, and called again. Wanda answered the phone and said, "I'm so sorry, but Maureen has just signed a contract to do a television show and will be traveling. Maureen is also completing a book, so she is only seeing parents who have lost children. But I can recommend someone we work with."

Desperate for help, I took the number and called her referral. I remember speaking with a woman who listened to me and was somewhat matter-of-fact about my plight. I knew at that moment that I had to meet Maureen and no one else. I thanked the woman, and hung up the phone. I again called Maureen's office, and asked for a ticket to see her at a local banquet hall where she was speaking in a few weeks.

A lady named Kelly handled the tickets. When I ordered them, I asked for an opportunity to meet Maureen.....nothing else. Kelly said she would see what she could do, with, of course, no promises.

A few weeks later, the time had arrived for Maureen's evening show. At this point in my life, my wife was planning on leaving me. We had been together for 22 years and we'd had three beautiful children together. But as I was to find out later when I met Maureen, she was on her own path, and nothing I did was going to change her or her thoughts and actions. So as it turned out, I went to the event alone.

As I entered, I saw a slender, young-looking lady at a table checking the guests in, and I immediately introduced myself. It was Kelly. She hugged me warmly, and again I stated that I would just like to meet Maureen, and again I got the same response, with a smile: "I'll see what I can do." I made my way to a large round banquet table. To my surprise, I was the only man sitting there with eight women. I exchanged pleasantries and waited, quietly scanning the room of approximately 25 tables.

The show began, and I caught my first glimpse of the famous Maureen Hancock: blonde, great smile, and full of energy. Maureen is something of a jokester and comedian, very animated and light in humor which made the mostly female crowd laugh. As the program progressed, Maureen would walk to various tables, explaining that she "tunes in" to those who have passed away from this world and moved to the next. As she drew near a table, she would start to talk and ask things like: "Who was Fred?" and one person at the table would respond, "He was my husband." Maureen would then tell the eager guest nearly everything about her deceased husband.

As a spectator, it was amazing to see the shock and awe on the family members' faces. I recall that one lady fainted when Maureen told her what her husband's nickname was. When she revived, the lady revealed that only she and her husband ever knew that secret. In all cases, Maureen would emphasize that the departed was "okay" in heaven, and that the person left behind on earth would soon be together with the deceased again. So many tears and laughs were exchanged it was almost indistinguishable at specific times.

As Maureen went from table to table, she would be drawn to one person or another, saying to all those present, "I have no control on whom, when, or where...it just happens." One particular table was directly across from mine, and as Maureen moved in that direction, she said, "I see a hat...with a badge of some sort... perhaps a policeman."

A few moments later, a younger lady who was sitting at the table started weeping and quietly said, "That hat was my dad's—he was an airline pilot. He gave me his hat before he passed away."

Maureen said, "He is proud of you! He knows you are writing a book. Keep at it!" The young girl nearly fell over, and had to be consoled by Maureen herself. I could see that she was deeply touched, because nobody knew of her writing endeavor, and she had started it after her Dad had passed away.

Near the end of the night, Maureen walked near our table, and as quickly as she did, she moved away, saying nothing to me or anyone else. For that matter, I don't believe she made eye contact with any of us. Shortly after that, the show concluded, and Maureen walked out of the room. I thought to myself, "Well, I guess it wasn't my time, or my turn, or whatever."

Just then, there was a tap on my shoulder. It was Kelly. She said: "Follow me."

I said, "Is she going to see me?"

She said, "Yes, you and only you."

I answered, "Does she normally see only one person after the show?"

Kelly replied, "Sometimes five or six. Tonight, just you."

At that moment an unspeakable calm came over me as I was led away to the far end of the banquet room to a corner behind a partition. There stood Maureen. What happened next was one of the most incredible experiences of my life.

I hugged her, then stepped back, looking right into her blue eyes; then I held out my hands and grasped hers. I said, "I'm George Popovici, and I have been very ill. I just wanted to meet you. I was told about you by my co-workers."

At that moment, Maureen closed her eyes, removed her right hand from my left, and held it high above her head, kind of shaking it by moving her wrist.

Without hesitation, I blurted out, "What are you doing?"

She replied, "You will be the highest of the high. You have a message, and you know you're different. Who is George?" she asked.

I said, "That is my paternal grandfather."

She said, "He says "hello." I was mesmerized by watching Maureen close her eyes, by her breathing during this moment. I told her that my grandfather had been a highly intelligent inventor who had studied at the Sorbonne in Paris, and later developed the synchronization equipment for motion pictures and sound at Paramount Studios in New York City. He had passed away in 1958, the year I was born.

I quickly took a minute to tell her about my maternal grandmother, Constantina, known to me as "Maia" (a Greek-rooted designation which is an honorific term for older women). I told Maureen how I used to visit my grandmother's country home in Massachusetts as a boy. In her large kitchen was an old cast-iron gas stove, a large kitchen table, a row of cabinets, an oversized porcelain sink, and a loveseat sofa that I used to sleep on.

As an Orthodox Christian, it was customary to have an "icon corner" or Iconostasis (Greek)—a small worship space prepared in the homes of Christians of the Eastern Orthodox tradition or Greek-Catholic Christians. Maia had lost her daughter, Juliana, when she was three weeks old and her son, Philip (for whom my brother is named), at seven years old. Instead of being bitter or depressed, in the early morning hours of each day my grand-mother would drop to her knees and face that devotional center, and pray prayers of thanksgiving for everything she still had.... and not focus on what she'd lost. I used to lie there in amazement.

My grandmother was a living saint on earth. I never heard her say a bad word toward anyone. She was the kindest and most loving person I have ever come to know on this earth, and I miss her terribly to this day. At that moment, Maureen opened her eyes and said, "I see the face of Jesus on her chest."

Maureen stared at my thin, broken frame, and said the words I longed to hear: "You need to come see me right away."

"YES!" I thought to myself. "I can finally know what my fate will be, find out if there is hope, and seek the reassurance I need to carry on." I hugged Maureen, and told her that I would call her assistant Wanda in the morning.

The next morning I called, and got Wanda on the phone. This kind and caring woman was as excited as I was to be able to see Maureen in a private setting. I could hear the anticipation in Wanda's voice as we spoke about finding a mutual time.

"I can't wait to meet you, George," Wanda said in a very calm and loving voice. "I just know that your angels made this possi-ble." I went silent. At that moment I could feel my grandmother and my ancestors swirling around me, and my body was tingling. I can't exactly explain it, but it felt like shocks all over my body, with images of my deceased loved ones in a circle over my head, in a bright light. I didn't dare tell this to Wanda or anyone else at the time—little did I know that if anyone would understand what I was seeing and feeling, it was Maureen and Wanda.

The day to meet Maureen came a week later. I drove into what looked like a strip mall with retail stores on the first floor and professional offices on the second. As I walked up the stairs, I was greeted by a smiling woman sitting at a reception desk with a warm "hello" and a big hug. Wanda is a taller lady with the face of an angel. She sat me down next to her desk, and held my hands.

"When you called the very first time, I just knew that I could help you," she said "See how it worked out? Your angels have put you here for a reason." I was tearing up at this point, because I knew what Wanda was telling me was true. She again reassured me that all of this was "meant to be," and to trust and believe.

Then she said, "Maureen is not here yet, but let's go into her healing room and get ready for her." I was led across the hall to a darker room that had a sliding door off the rear with a view of the woods. The room was painted in soft tones, with two chairs facing each other in one corner. Lined around the room were photos of children who had passed away—scores of photos of angelic faces that had left this life to go to eternity. Near the two chairs was a tape recorder. Wanda told me that Maureen would soon be there.

I recall vividly that it was a cloudy day, so the room was fairly dark. Wanda took the opportunity to open the blinds of the sliding door to brighten the room. She then walked over and held a blank cassette tape to her chest.

"Does George need this?" she asked out loud. She stood motionless for a moment with her eyes closed and took a deep breath. "Yes."

With that, she loaded the tape into the recorder.

I asked her, "Who did you ask?"

She replied, "Your Angels." Wanda then took a little bundle of sage grass and lit it with a match. She walked around the room as if she had the Olympic torch in her hand.

Of course I asked, "What are you doing?"

Wanda smiled, replying, "This is to cleanse the room." I said nothing further, and sat patiently as she completed her task. She asked me if I wanted anything, and then said that Maureen would be in shortly.

I stayed seated in the chair and waited for Maureen to arrive. While sitting there, I scanned the photos of children of all ages positioned about the room. Directly in front of me was a small table with a statue of the Holy Mother (Virgin Mary) on it. Around the statue was a set of beautiful rosary prayer beads. I stared at the statue and quietly asked God for help with all of my struggles. Within a minute, Maureen came in, and we hugged. She took her seat directly across from mine, and we got right to it. Maureen commented on how good I looked. She was all smiles, and looking very full of life with her blonde hair up, and wearing an exercise suit and colorful sneakers.

Maureen stared at me, and held my hands for a moment. She leaned over and started the tape recorder.

"You really don't need this, because you will remember all that is significant as we speak."

I asked her to go ahead and activate the recorder after I made one statement. I started by saying, "Maureen, do you see that photograph behind me?" and before she could answer, I said, "That is the image of my life, all in a frame: my wife, my children, and my profession. It is all fading and crumbling, as if that picture has fallen off the wall and crashed to the floor. I feel like there is nothing left." I hung my head and started to sob.

Maureen turned on the recorder and said, "George, listen to me. I want you to take yourself out of that picture for a moment and see that there is a much larger one. Everything you are experiencing is for a reason...everything happens for a reason. You are different, and you know you are. You have an important message to share. You walk up to strangers and they are captivated by your messages of hope and truth, yet you see yourself as a piece of garbage. Your illness, your wife's decisions, and what has transpired and what is about to happen and will happen in the future is in a plan. You are heartbroken and sad. Stop thinking that way...you have so much to offer!

"When you step back and understand the larger picture, you will be able come to terms with the fact that you are on your own path. Your parents, wife, children, friends, relatives, and colleagues are all on *their own* paths, too. You have a purpose, and you must fulfill that purpose." I sat there, half-stunned.

Then reverting to the thinking she had just told me to disregard, I regressed with another round of,"Maureen, I love my wife, and I want her to know how much I love her. What about my family, our home, and all we have built? The thought of losing it is too much for me. As a matter of fact, I planned to see my son at his University a month ago. Two weeks later we met. I decided when planning the visit that this trip to visit would be a perfect cover to end my life that night. I knew that the roads leading to his campus were dark and winding. Crashing my car into a grove of large trees on a hairpin corner a mile or so away from his campus would look like an accident. Why shouldn't I do it? My life has crumbled...there is no hope. The day soon arrived, and I went up to my son's dorm room and ordered a few pizzas. I sat there most unemotionally letting my son know just how much I loved him as we ate. I told him that I supported him and was proud of him. It was getting late, and it was a particularly rainy and foggy night. Perfect, I thought to myself. It will look as if it was an accident.

"As I was about to say goodbye, my son turned to me and said, 'Dad, please be careful. It's late and I know you can't see too well anymore. Please, Dad, I love you.' Oh my God, I thought. What was I to do now? If I did go through with it, my son would have felt all the guilt of that night forever! My mind raced for a moment. I hugged him and told him, 'I'll see you later.' As I left the campus parking lot, I pondered the guilt that would befall my firstborn son if I carried out my plan. He would have been the last to see his Dad. As I turned out of that lot and slowly passed the location I had selected for my 'accident' to happen, I knew, I just knew that no matter the pain I was feeling, I could not inflict that on my children."

Maureen then looked me right in the eye, and said, "Oh my God...Oh my God. Had you done that, you would have been taken to the next set of lessons here on earth. I see you would have hit the trees and would have survived. I see you in a bed with a paintbrush in your mouth as a quadriplegic. Oh, my God."

Now I was speechless and in shock. Maureen took a few moments to compose herself, and then looked at me directly again, and said, "I cannot become emotional, George, or I will lose my connection. I know the pain you have been feeling...the hopelessness and despair. Remember that you are in a rented car, George. The body you are in is temporary. Your spirit is who you are. All that happens is pre-determined. You need constant reassurance. Remember, you are special and exceptional. You have a message to give."

At that moment the tone of the entire meeting changed. I sat there, still in shock but fully aware that what Maureen was saying was the gospel truth. I had known what she was talking about, but never quite understood it. In retrospect, I can recall what a dear friend of mine, Rose Barboza, (who also has a story in this book), had told me: "God loves you so much he has chosen you to suffer for others." That concept makes all the sense in the world to me today, because I would not have thought about writing this book without the experience I went through. I would have never met Maureen. None of it would have mattered.

I asked Maureen, "How will I help others?"

She replied, "You have known things all your life. You may write a book to get your message out." She continued, "Remember that guy who passed and came back—he was on Oprah. He was famous and had a message. Well, I see you like him...getting your message out."

At the time, I was in such shock that my mind could not scan the list of famous deceased speakers fast enough. I later concluded that it was Randy Pausch, who authored the "Last Lecture" months before his death. The amazing thing is, that book was given to me long before I met Maureen by a fishing buddy of mine. He thought it would give me inspiration through all that I was enduring. That was another God moment for sure.

I asked Maureen, "Do you see us working together?"

She replied, "I saw it as soon as I sat down." I was reeling from what I had just heard, knowing that God had connected me "directly" with his plan through the famous Maureen Hancock. I knew I was meant to tell my story, in the hope that my experience would help and inspire others.

Part I

My Story

CHAPTER 1

The Fall

"Never, Never, Never Give Up"
Winston Churchill

My odyssey began in October 2005 when I started to feel pains in my groin and legs. I quickly made an appointment with my local primary care doctor, who happened to be a social friend of mine. I spoke to this man, whom I called "Doc," with confidence about my difficulties—after all, throughout my entire life I had been in command of any and all crises. My belief that I could deal with this matter came from my experience as an emergency medical technician, a firefighter in my early years, and later in my current career as a safety engineer. (Safety Engineers solve all types of complex and technical problems.) As with all engineers, we are trained to believe that there is a logical solution for every problem: A+B=C, and so I thought we would easily find a solution to my medical issue as well.

Like most healthy Americans, I did not spend much time in doctors' offices or medical facilities. As a matter of fact, I avoided them like the plague. The notion of wasting any more of my precious life having an annual physical and hanging around a germ-infested waiting room with folks who were ill was completely repulsive to me. I felt I was far too important to my family and to those who I served in my work and in the community. When I first became ill, I was taken aback. "I am George Popovici," I told myself, "and this can't be happening to me."

Doc ran the usual blood tests, and based on my symptoms, he deduced that I had a prostate infection known as prostatitis. He prescribed a one-month course of heavy-duty antibiotics, which is the standard course of treatment for a malady of this nature. By Thanksgiving, a month later, I was very weak. Mind you, I was a 5'9" 145-pound powerhouse of energy. I could outpace most men my age, and run with the best of them. I played with my kids, and enjoyed outrunning them whenever possible. As a matter of fact, I was "the Dad that could." I deep-sea fished, swam, downhill-skied, hiked, white-water-rafted, hunted, exercised regularly with weights and rode my bike. But I was barely able to stand while attending a charity auction in early December, and, in fact, I had to sit through the entire event.

I had confidence in Doc, but knew deep down after the third clinical visit and associated laboratory tests that whatever was happening to me was highly unusual and very abnormal. Having been a healthy person all of my life, I knew my body, and what felt right and wrong. *This was definitely wrong.* I knew I should be starting to improve at this point, but the weakness and pain persisted. As a matter of fact, the pain had started to turn into a burning sensation in my thighs.

For the first time in my life, I began to doubt. Could the weakness have been a reaction to the antibiotics? Did I do more damage by taking the "big gun" pharmacological prescription? Why should I ask myself such questions? After all, I had faith in the medical community, and had no reason to question or doubt any medical professional. As an educated engineer, I understood the scientific advances made in medical science, knew many doctors socially, and listened to them speak of the new research or treatment regimens appearing for the benefit of their patients. Surely Doc could find the underlying cause of my problem and order the proper treatment so I could get back to my very busy life.

Christmas was almost upon us, and we had to get the house ready for the kids. My firstborn son Nicholas was 14 at the time, my daughter Alexandra was 12, and little Gregory was 10. We were right in the thick of social events surrounding the holidays and planning winter activities.

On my fourth office visit, just before Christmas 2005, Doc told me he really did not have a clear clinical picture as to what was happening to me. My joints had started to ache excruciatingly every time I moved. Thankfully, my work is primarily in an office setting, so I was able to make my normal 75-minute commute and sit at my desk for most of the day. Walking to and from my car was a challenge, as I huffed and puffed. I had to carry my laptop computer and other critical safety data with me every day in case I was called on in the off hours of my job.

Doc finally sent me to a local hospital to test for Lyme disease, and simultaneously referred me to a rheumatologist friend of his in a neighboring community, Dr. Marcy, who he felt would have more in-depth specific training in obscure diseases. Sadly, I was told it would take me three months to see Dr. Marcy.

For those of you not familiar with Lyme disease, it is a bacterial infection in which spirochetes bore into the muscle tissue causing tremendous joint pain, neurological problems, and weakness. Left untreated, it can be fatal. Three months into the illness, my tests for the disease came back negative. What many doctors do not know about this insidious disease is that the standard testing is not always conclusive. Depending on the stage of the disease, it can show as negative on various tests.

Over the holidays, I spoke with family and friends as well as other physicians I was acquainted with. All of them urged me "not to fool around" and to get to a Boston Hospital. After all, Boston is a major city, with the oldest university in the nation. Extending my care to a city hospital was an idea that did not appeal to me, because I was attempting to continue a "normal" routine. My health problem was shameful to me for a host of reasons. The New Year was on the horizon, and I had big projects planned at work. My boss at the time was a good-hearted man; however, he was trained in the US Army and had retired as a full Colonel. Although he did not say it, I knew he wanted me to "adapt and overcome" by keeping a stiff upper lip and bearing it out....and believe me, I felt the same way! My symptoms had reached a point where I finally had a sit-down with him, and told him I had a health issue but that I expected to rapidly resolve it. He supported my plan, and released me from work over the next few weeks so I could get to the bottom of the illness.

"Okay," I thought, "now that I have a plan, who do I see? Where do I go?" There are many hospitals in Boston. Right then and there, I knew that I would have to advocate for myself. If you have not ever been in that space, it can be daunting, frustrating, lonely, and downright scary.

While I was at work, I confided in a well-respected colleague. Mary is a young, successful, vibrant co-worker at my company, amazing in her outlook and spirit. She always hugs me when we meet, and generally has a smile on her face. I certainly consider her a role model.

The way I became acquainted with Mary was unusual, to say the least. I was walking the floor of a safety conference trade show in 2004 in Orlando. I started a conversation with a vendor who sold Automated External Defibrillators (AED's). When the vendor asked where I worked and I told him, he replied, "I am Mary's brother." After listening to his sales pitch, I emailed Mary to introduce myself and tell her of my chance meeting. Little did I know that she in a year she would become a lifeline angel for me.

I have come to understand that there are angels all around us all the time. We don't often recognize them because we are too caught up in our daily routine, or we brush their messages off as coincidence. I am firmly convinced that Mary's brother led me to her for a reason. This was my introduction to the angels who circled me and guided me as I fell further into ill health.

Now, before you think I have had one too many pharmacological injections, I will tell you that I was as skeptical as anyone at this point in my life. I am an engineer. I lived squarely in the linear, physical world, and have always reverted to the simple formula of A+B=C. It was incredible to me that these kinds of "coincidences" keep presenting themselves in my life.

Mary has been diagnosed with a chronic illness. She has a debilitating inflammatory disease that primarily affects the joints and other organs of the body. Mary was being seen by a doctor whom she raved about, and she believed he could shed light on my advancing condition. His name was Dr. Roberts, and he practiced at one of the most prominent hospitals in America. Mary gave me Dr. Roberts' name, and she also called her contact who was able to arrange a speedy appointment with this doctor, who was in great demand.

At this point, I couldn't believe that my health could fail, or that I could become this ill this quickly and not get any answers. I was used to getting answers to my questions quickly. My symptoms had progressed to the point that I was so weak I could barely walk; I developed visual difficulties; my skin was getting mysteriously darker; and I noticed flashing lights when I closed my eyes.

I intentionally minimized my situation to my wife, the commander of our home's day-to-day operations. I felt that having her worry would only make matters worse at home and the worry and wait had really taken a toll. I had an appointment set for January 15th, 2006, and thankfully the holidays were behind us. I could focus on getting to the cause of my failing health.

Dr. Roberts was a seasoned, well-respected doctor. He listened patiently to me as I explained the expanding constellation of symptoms. I think he was truly receptive until I broke down emotionally. I started to weep like a child. He was polite and kind, but suspected that my illness was more of a psychological infirmity than an organic medical condition. The pressure to find an answer and get back to normal business had taken its toll, right there in his Boston exam room.

Dr. Roberts assured me that he would be back to me within a week. When the week had come and gone, I called. As with many practices, the nurse relays the laboratory findings to the patient, especially if the doctor has a busy practice or does not want to deal with the patient. In my case, I suspected the latter. At that time, the only abnormal labs were elevated protein in my blood and a higher-than-normal C Reactive Protein (CRP), which is a marker of inflammation. When I questioned the nurse, she felt it was not a matter of concern per the doctor's note, and said that he would not need to see me again. Conversely, when I called my local doc to get a second opinion, he indicated that these were significant findings. "Oh, great," I thought, "now what do I do?"

This was my first encounter with a major medical facility, and I found it sadly lacking. I felt rejected and perplexed.

CHAPTER 2

Beginning The Search for Answers

"Success is not final, failure is not fatal:
it is the courage to continue that counts."
Winston Churchill

I knew now that I had a real medical issue, and I needed to get answers. I have never quit on any matter in my life, and as a matter of fact, I have always strived to achieve excellence if at all possible. I was a hard worker, I was competitive, and I was an achiever—not to mention the head of the household. As capable as my family was, my kids needed me. Here I was, fighting an unknown illness for four months, with no answers, and my condition was worsening.

In February, my breathing became affected, and my heart felt like it was going to come straight though my chest. As exhausted as I was, I could not sleep much. I tried all types of prescription sleep aids, but I still couldn't get more than three hours of sleep. What I didn't know is that the Lyme disease had already rooted itself in my brain and GI Tract, and was beginning to disable my normal body functions, specifically my autonomic nervous system. I made three more trips to the local hospital's emergency room in January and February. I found it humiliating to be in a "john-nie" and stuck with needles and probes in every part of my body. Once I was so upset and weak that I called 911 to have the rescue services transport me so I could obtain faster service at the ER.

I was told by a friend of my wife that this was "All in my head," and that I was making myself sick. As it turns out, she was not completely incorrect. Many physicians now understand the importance of a strong attitude, of belief in healing (having

23

a will and purpose to live) with regard to any illness. They have finally accepted that the body is an integrated system, and that illness of any type affects the entire organism.

I continued to work full time. On my way to work one morning on a slick stretch of highway not far from my home, I suddenly felt dizzy and disoriented. I lost control of my car—it spun around 360 degrees three times, and went off the road, hitting a tree on the opposite side of the road. Shaken, I called my wife, who worked nearby, for a ride. I called my boss, informing him of my mishap. She and my boss conferred privately, and decided that it might be best if I took a few weeks off to relax and gather my thoughts. Remember, I did not have a definitive diagnosis at that time. Needless to say, I had destroyed the car, and was very depressed.

I began to believe that it was indeed "all in my head," so I checked into the hospital for a four-day evaluation of my psychological health. I admitted to myself, after crying on and off for nearly two months, that I was now feeling hopeless about my situation. I felt that I had I let my family down and that I had I abandoned my employer and the employees I served. This was my first hard hit on rock bottom.

The attending psychiatrist met with me, and told me that I should not feel hopeless. He suggested that I go home and battle my illness without shame. He prescribed anti-depressants, which I never took. I had never even taken an aspirin before I became ill, never a pill for anything. I didn't drink coffee, smoke, or gamble. I was George Popovici, and this could not be happening to me! I would not yield and would not be dissuaded.

During my third and last trip to the local ER, I was subjected to the same battery of tests, IV's, waiting, and more waiting. Nurses hooked me up to the cardiac monitor, took CT scans of my abdomen, and took many blood and urine tests. Still, there was nothing specific. They had no explanation for why I was ill.

I decided right then and there that I had to take charge of my health MYSELF. Our family had a preferred health plan, and I could select any specialist as required without preauthorization. If I was going down, I was going down my way...swinging. Little did I know how dizzying, complex, and draining the process is to research doctors, facilities, procedures, possible diagnoses, and other resources. I would soon become a master at booking appointments, compiling medical records, and coordinating communications with various specialists.

Thus came the development of the "football"—a nickname I affectionately use to refer to my carry-along medical records file. The term comes from the fact that the President of the United States has a military aide that travels with him at all times, carrying the nuclear launch codes in a secured briefcase. That briefcase is handcuffed to the aide, and nicknamed the "football." By now, my "football" was two inches thick, with reports, labs, and summary notes in chronological order from onset of illness to present—just as an engineer should operate, in perfect synchronous order.

While in the ER, I was seen by a cardiologist and a local gastroenterologist (both happened to be acquaintances from the private Catholic school that our children had previously attended). In the interim, I decided that I would contact another local physician pal who was an infectious disease doc, who I was acquainted with in the same manner, and who happened to practice in the same hospital as the cardiologist.

Now I thought there was hope! I was going to get answers! "I have all my pals on the case, I thought, "so who needs Boston now?" Little did I know that this was the beginning of the most complex pinball game anyone could ever play!

My cardiologist's son had played sports at school with my son Nick. We socialized with the family on occasion, and I felt very comfortable with the doctor and his style. He saw me locally, and asked me to come to his city office for testing which was forty minutes from my home. Before I knew it, I was wired like a Christmas tree and running on a treadmill. I was then put in a device that scanned my heart. As with all the docs, I had to wait for him to call me back, albeit a short few days. Then the news came directly from him.

"George, your right heart ventricle is hypertrophic," he stated, which meant it was twice as large as it should be, "and we don't know why. Could be a viral cardiomyopathy. We aren't really certain."

"Okay, what do I do, doc?" I asked.

"Nothing, we just monitor it," he replied.

"ARE YOU KIDDING ME?" I thought. "I want answers."

I was given a small monitor to wear on my belt, not once, but twice, to observe abnormal behavior of the heart. He wanted me back for additional testing.

I was spending a lot of time trying to line up tests to cover as many bases as I could to find the reason for my accelerating deterioration. In March, my hands had started to tremble, and my face twitched. So without further hesitation, I called work and told them that again, I would have to be out for a while.

The reality that I was in for a protracted fight began to set in. Yes, a fight. That's what dealing with a chronic disease is like. What's more, if you don't have a diagnosis, you're chopped liver to the doctors who don't want to be bothered ordering tests upon tests. Insurance coverage is spotty for an undefined illness. Thankfully, I work for a great company. My integrity was never questioned at work. I had won company and national recognition awards for my forward advancements in safety both at our firm and in the industry. I received one hundred percent support from everyone, including executive team members.

I met Dr. Flanders, a tall Irish man and a great human being. He and his wife had had four kids, and adopted another. I met with him in his office, and let him know that I had been ill for nearly five months. I showed him my previous labs. Could he please perform all the tests known to man on me?

"Please help me," I pleaded. He performed a multitude of tests that came up blank. I started to tear up again because the pains in my groin and legs had intensified. My abdomen was tender and slightly swollen. Yet his tests showed no abnormalities.

Then came Dr. Masters, a quiet and humble man. His wife was active in the private school sector, and a real saint of a woman. They had a large family, and were very active in the school. Dr.

Masters was a gastroenterologist, and a good one at that. I told him that I thought I was bleeding rectally. He saw me in his office and confirmed the same. He suggested I have a colonoscopy as soon as possible and I agreed.

After the procedure, Dr. Masters told me that he had removed an adenomas polyp from my colon. These types of polyps are precancerous, and can be dangerous if undetected or left in place. I questioned him at length as to whether or not that could have been the cause of all my symptoms. He was very doubtful, so with that I was released, and went home to recover.

Six hours later, I awoke to excruciating pain in the exact spot where the polyp had been snared. I had no idea where the polyp had been located, and didn't find out the pain was located there until later. I called the doc at home and woke him up, explained what was happening and where. I believe he was in disbelief at first.

"It was very routine," he said. "I saw no complications." And with that, he instructed me to head directly back to the ER. As soon as I got there, they started an IV and scanned my abdomen. I was running a 103-degree fever. Something was happening! Dr. Masters arrived the next morning. Overnight tests revealed that I had a bacterial infection, possibly as a result of the snared polyp. The doctors did not know the cause, but I'll never forget Dr. Master's words that day: "We need to get to the bottom of this," he said.

They admitted me to the hospital, and started me on a course of broad-spectrum antibiotics. The hospitalist, Dr. Dimo, was brilliant and very thorough. I was assigned a beautiful private room in our local, modern hospital. Dr. Dimo held me for 24 hours, until the white cell count in my blood started to normalize. That was good news!

Something was working, I thought...Thank God. Thank God. I was released and went home.

CHAPTER 3
Cheerleading Angel

"Be kind, for everyone you meet
is fighting a harder battle."
Plato

It was the end of March 2006. Snow covered the ground, and it was cold. I stayed in bed for four days. During that time I had a few visitors. One in particular that stands out was Jane Smith, a tall blond lady married to our investment advisor. Jane was a stay-at-home mom who tutored my oldest boy, Nicholas. I will never forget hearing the doorbell and opening it to see this full-smiled woman with a tray of home-cooked dinner for our family that evening. She had a note and flower attached. That was it. I lost it right then and there in front of her. She just hugged me and comforted me.

I rapidly became weaker and weaker. I could not walk to my mailbox. The once vibrant and strong son, husband, and dad was reduced to a bedridden dishrag. I lost significant weight, and at one point I was down to 125 lbs. As much as I forced myself to eat, I could not gain weight. One day in April, I got a massive headache that would not go away, and I started to see flashing lights and black spots in my vision.

God and His angels must have been with me. I called the local hospital back and asked for Dr. Dimo. By a stroke of luck, he called me back. I explained my worsening condition in detail to Dr. Dimo. Without hesitation, he instructed me to return to the ER.

"Doctor, you know my case is complex," I pleaded, '...please help me!' He said he would "find a bed for me." He was going to admit me on an emergency basis due to my hospitalization just a week earlier - a small miracle in today's medical world.

And so began again what I thought would be the start of the end of all my problems. I was frightened and perplexed by all these unexplained symptoms and abnormalities. Was it a rare cancer? Some strange disease? Was I crazy? What was happening to me? On that cool April day I drove myself to the hospital. Again, I went through the process of paperwork, checking in and waiting.

Extremely weak, I welcomed any and all testing planned by Dr. Dimo. True to his word, the barrage of testing began. He first ordered a CT scan of the chest, STAT, based on a hunch. (STAT is a medical term that means immediately.) This test involved my lying on a table while a large donut-shaped X-RAY bombarded me with gamma rays to obtain an image of the area being surveyed. In my case, it was the heart and lungs. That's not bad at all, but here is the corker: you need to be injected with an iodine serum that highlights the image in order to contrast any abnormality. I was warned by the nurses that the serum might cause a physical reaction.

After a barrage of questions regarding allergic reactions, etc., they commenced the test. Halfway through, they indicated that they were going to remotely inject the dye, and I might feel "warm." Not only was I warm, it felt like a blowtorch was put on every part of my body. I broke out in a cold sweat, and felt sick enough to vomit. The nurses observed my reaction and wanted to stop the test. I refused, and demanded they continue in my quest for answers. Within minutes of being wheeled back to my room, nurses showed up adding intravenous bags and injections of various meds for my IV line. Of course, I questioned them and they replied, "Ask Dr. Dimo."

One hour after the test, Dr. Dimo himself came into my room and said: "You have a small pulmonary embolism (PE) in the left lung. Your blood is clotting."

I replied: "This must be a bad dream...are you certain?" Dr. Dimo knew I had been through hell, so he took a moment to put the films up on the view light. All the time, his pager was beeping and his cell phone ringing. He pointed carefully to the spot in the lung.

"I suspected this when you called," he said. "We are starting a Heparin IV and Lovenox injections in the abdomen. You will also have to start with warfarin (Coumadin) to thin your blood. We don't know what is causing your blood to clot, but we'll start testing for an answer now." He also said, "You may have to be on blood thinners for the rest of your life." I later found out that a PE can often be fatal if the clot moves out of the lung and into the artery. So I was lucky.

"Should I be happy?" I wondered. "Sad? Panicked?" I didn't know. "Okay," I said to myself, "They have found something and this may be the springboard to getting to the bottom of this entire illness."

Tests included an MRI of the brain, CT scans, neurological tests, and the like. At this point, a mid-line was installed in my arm to receive fluids and other medications as required. A mid-line is a plastic line that is inserted in your vein with a plastic cap on the end of it. The cap is connected to the liquid medications when needed. Sadly, every time blood is drawn, nurses cannot use the line due to the liquid medications in the line, so, you guessed it: needle sticks over and over again. Nurses and assistants came in every two hours on the dot.

"Sorry to wake you, Mr. Popovici, but...." Before they could finish, I politely said, "Could I please sleep another few hours, please!" Then the routine of sticking and drawing blood started all over again.

Symptom-wise I could feel my back starting to ache, not shooting pains, but an ache. Dr. Dimo ordered an MRI of my spine. My temperature started to fall below 98.6 degrees—somewhere in the neighborhood of 96.5—and believe me, I was cold. I had three or four blankets over me at all times. I repeatedly asked the nurses if they could increase the room temperature, which they did, but I was always cold. What few doctors know is that most Lyme-ridden patients have low internal temperatures that develop when the infection wreaks havoc on the central nervous system. Additionally, I started to bleed from my nose.

Another doctor I knew, an Ear-Nose-and-Throat specialist, Dr. Sam Foster, came to visit, examine me, and review my MRI films. He indicated that I had infected sinuses, and suggested more antibiotics. Herein was the genesis of my neurological symptoms, as my autonomic nervous system and brain began to be affected by my disease. Although the doctors had no idea exactly what was wrong with me, they knew it was complex and unusual, just as I had suspected.

The word got out in our little town that I was in the hospital. I started to receive telephone calls, along with two visitors who may have changed my attitude about the entire affair. I was feeling very low, but had a small bit of hope in Dr. Dimo's assurance that he would leave "no stone unturned." This was the beginning of my true journey for medical answers on a larger playing field. What I didn't know was that this was the genesis of my awakening as a human being to a much larger, broader, and perhaps incomprehensible aspect of life.

During my stay, my first cheerleading angel appeared: Marcia Blackburn. I had known Marcia for 10 years at that point, but did not specifically socialize with her or see her on any frequent basis. A black-haired woman with piercing blue eyes and a belly laugh that would make Santa Claus envious, she was the director of the day-care center our kids attended while we worked.

I had always admired Marcia's drive and charisma. She is married to Bill Blackburn, a great, easygoing guy. They have four little girls. Marcia saw that I was in a bad way, physically and mentally. She knew just by looking at me that the vibrant man she knew had been reduced to a bedridden bag of bones.

She walked in one quiet morning, and in a cheery voice she said, "Hey, how're you doing?" I was ecstatic that she had taken the time to visit. As we started talking, I became emotional again. I told Marcia that I felt I'd made mistakes, and that I had failed my family. That saint of a woman held my hand for an hour telling me that everyone's lives have issues, and not to blame myself for anything. You see, because of her own life issues, Marcia learned that a person's view of the world and their mental state have a direct relationship on behavior and physical wellbeing.

This was something I had not been exposed to before. My life had always been goal-oriented, with the next target always in the crosshairs. I believe now that the reason I focused continually on goals was to bolster my deep insecurity and fear that if I relaxed, I would not be viewed by my wife and children as the husband/father that did them right. I had been an altar boy and Eagle Scout, and active in local youth associations and charitable boards, but I had never felt it was enough.

Marcia told me in no uncertain terms, "Let go, George, and let God." Looking back as recently as October of 2009, I can honestly say that I knew that was what I should do, but I could not completely accept it. My engineering training and the structured life programming I had always lived by was too strong to convert. A+B=C was alive and well! Having said that, it's important to communicate that I have always believed in God. I have always known that life is not an accident. When Marcia said those words, I got a glimpse of what it was to have an angel appear in your life to deliver a message. Although I did not fully comprehend it at the time, I did appreciate it deeply, because it gave me the strength to face the next challenge in the search for answers.

Dr. Dimo was a sharp, young detective doctor. I sensed that he truly wanted to find the answer, and I prayed that he would and could. I became numb to all the poking and prodding. It didn't matter at this point. I needed and wanted answers. Dr. Dimo came in daily to update me on the opinions of the wagon-train of specialists he had ordered to see me.

Of course, my family came in the evenings. The kids were shaken to see Dad in a hospital bed, with wires and tubes attached. After all, I was their father. I kept it positive and upbeat, keeping myself together for them until time for the goodbyes. Nick had to leave the room sometimes, sobbing. I felt sick to my stomach. I was so empty and sad. I knew I had to press on, and kept reminding myself over and over that I had a great responsibility to them. That was the driving reason to carry on.

While I was in limbo on day #3, my second angel appeared in the afternoon. His name is Brad Peters. Brad is an educated, well-to-do man that insures yachts. Interestingly, his son was a classmate of my youngest son, Gregory, years before at the day-care center that Marcia commanded.

Brad brought me a book to read on the history of tuna fishing, which included techniques to catch big game tuna. As I've lived near the ocean my entire life, I love to tuna fish and this was a real treat. Brad knew deep down from his own experience that I needed a distraction. His dad had spent a time in the hospital with a terminal illness, and Brad recalled how important it was for him to focus on anything other than his illness. He told me how he sometimes asked the nurses to allow his dad to sip a beer and eat a slice of pizza. Of course this was strictly forbidden under hospital policy, but Brad was persuasive, and he and his dad enjoyed a beer in the hospital room. Shortly thereafter, Brad's father passed away.

Brad had quietly survived a divorce when his son was a little tot. He has since remarried a beautiful young lady and they have two additional boys. Brad made it a point to encourage me every time I see him. His comments always ended with: "Remember there is light at the end of the tunnel." I reflect on that daily. Thank you, Brad!

My parents, Richard and Flora Popovici, had called me during my first hospital stay. They live in Florida in the winter months, and have done so for decades. My dad is a highly intelligent man who had become successful with very little help—self-made all the way. Dad was born in the USA, but left to go back to Europe as a young man with his parents, George and Ecaterina Popovici.

When Dad was age six and living in New York City, he was given sulfa-based drugs, to which he was allergic. The result was serious nerve damage to his motor functions. As a result, his hand and head tremble in a way similar to a person who is diagnosed with Parkinson's Disease. His physical affliction did nothing to his sharp mind. Dad was very savvy regarding medical techniques and advancements, in part for his own preservation.

We had a discussion regarding my case. As luck would have it, one of my dad's friends from his church in Florida was a retired Doctor of Pain Management, having practiced at a famed clinic in Ohio. His name is Dr. David Thomas. Dad was troubled that I did not have a diagnosis, and offered to discuss my case in detail with Dr. Thomas. Dad called me later that week, and instructed me to call Dr. Thomas, which I did.

Dr. Thomas, a super-bright, compassionate man, quickly explained to me that the "practice of medicine" was just that. "It's as much an art as it is a science," he stated. This was my first exposure to the abstract aspects of medicine. I suspected that Dr. Thomas told me that because he knew that I had been suffering and searching for answers. Like most people in the world, I expected to have quick answers from the highly advanced medical establishment in this great nation.

As I listened carefully, he mentioned several complex cases which were not easily resolved at the clinic, and were referred to a famous, high-profile private practice doctor in New York City, Dr. Ralph Brown. He also made it a point to let me know that if I saw doctors like that, it was going to be expensive.

"Great medical help in these circumstances costs a lot," he said. I never forgot that, and boy, was he right. I repeatedly thanked Dr. Thomas for his efforts.

The morning of the fifth day of my hospital stay arrived, and Dr. Dimo made an early visit to my room.

"We can't find anything significant beyond your PE," he stated—not the news I wanted to hear. At that time I actually pleaded with him to keep probing and testing.

"At this point, we have performed many tests," he said. "I cannot make a diagnosis." I told him that I intended to see the doctor in New York City, and asked him what his thoughts were. He said: "I cannot tell you what to do and where to go. Good luck." I thanked him for believing in me and extending himself to admit me.

I was not in a good frame of mind. It was April 2005, I was not working, major projects at the office were being undertaken without me, and I was still very ill. My beloved major-league baseball season was about to start, and I could have cared less. All I wanted to do was get well and resume my life with my wife and family.

CHAPTER 4

New Possibilities

*"When you come to the end of your rope,
tie a knot and hang on."*
Franklin D. Roosevelt

Home again, I called the office of Dr. Brown. Dr. Brown, I came to find out, is quite famous. He was known as an "out-of-the-box" thinker. He authored many books on wellness, and had a radio and television program in the New York metropolitan area, as well as an extensive website that identified him as a director of certain medical foundations. That gave me a degree of hope.

Dr. Brown's office indicated that I would need three days to complete the testing. I begged and pleaded to see him as soon as possible. As luck would have it, they had a cancellation on the following Tuesday. I took the appointment. I arranged to take the Amtrak Acela train from Providence to New York. I stayed at the Carlton Hotel on Madison Avenue. I figured if I was going to kick the bucket, I was going to do it in style.

To this point, all that I had been responsible for on my very costly medical treatments and tests were the co-payments. Dr. Brown's office was my first experience with the process of paying up front, and then submitting the payment to the insurance company for reimbursement. We had plenty of money, and I continued to earn a full salary while out of work.

The train ride was uneventful, and I arrived in the afternoon. I was extremely weak at this point. I recall trying to stand in the cab line at Penn Station to get a cab to the Carlton Hotel. I was wobbling, and needed a rail to keep myself from falling. I was staring down 43rd Street at the Empire State Building, and watching it sway to and fro. What was happening to me? How could this be happening?

I checked into the hotel. I sat on my bed and broke down crying. I could not believe this. Again, I asked myself: "Is this a bad dream?" And of course, the same repeated question: "Why?" I attempted to walk to a deli recommended by the concierge a few blocks away. Mistake! It literally took me an hour to walk three blocks and back. Now I *knew* I was in trouble. I honestly felt that I would not leave the city. I spent that first night in New York in my luxurious hotel room alone. I was weak, tired, sick, and very, very sad. Tomorrow was another day, and I had to gather the strength to have hope that Dr. Brown could do what six months of exhaustive testing and eleven doctors could not.

I arrived at Dr. Brown's office, which was situated in an older office building on Madison Avenue, at 9 a.m. sharp. I was asked to complete a plethora of forms and paperwork, as was standard fare with most physicians. The waiting room was full of potential patients. Some were visibly ill, others not. Then I was shuttled into the business office, where I was asked what method of payment I preferred. I explained that I did have medical insurance that was of the highest quality. I struck an agreement to pay for half of the visit and have them direct-bill the other half.

Soon after, I was sent to an interview room with a nurse. All the information I had amassed to this point was turned over to her. She skimmed over it briefly, and asked many questions on the history of this illness, and my family history. I then started an "assembly line" of testing: 24 vials of blood, urine tests, bone scans, brain scans, memory testing, ultrasound imaging, etc. Taking blood was a challenge now. My veins had retracted deep into my arms, as they are today. The medical director herself had to draw the vials after four attempts.

I was promised that at some point during the day I would see Dr. Brown. Sure enough, at the end of the day I saw him for 20 minutes. He reviewed a few of the real-time tests. Dr. Brown was a strong believer in Human Growth Hormone (HGH). It was his opinion that no matter what the root cause of my illness was, the HGH would bolster the body.

He told me, "It costs $2,000 per month. We supply it, and you'll learn to inject it yourself. You are looking at $50,000.00 for the treatment and follow-ups."

"Okay," I said. "I'll take that into consideration, Dr. Brown." Before I left, they had me stop at the supplements desk and pick up a shopping bag full of bottles that cost a cool $989. At the end of the day, I decided to try to walk back to my hotel, ten blocks away. You guessed it. One and a half hours later I made it to the elevator, went up to my room, and collapsed.

The next day was much the same as the first, with one exception: I had a meeting with Dr. Brown's medical director. Evidently, some of the testing had come back, and showed an abnormal CRP protein in the blood—surprise!—and then again, low DHEA, which is the major secretory steroidal product of the adrenal glands, and is also produced by the gonads and the brain. DHEA (Dehydroepiandrosterone) is the most abundant circulating steroid in humans.

The medical director said, "You are fighting something, but we really don't know what."

The next morning at 11 a.m., Dr. Brown met me to again advocate for HGH. He also suggested a bevy of supplements which were privately labeled for his practice by a well-known pharmaceutical firm. The total cost, with hotel and a two-day stay, was $14,000. Fortunately for us, I had a lucrative consulting business. I could cover most medical expenses from that account. Back on the train heading home, I tried to collect my thoughts, and wondered what had just happened to me. In fact, I was pondering whether or not I would ever find answers and halt my decline.

At this point, I was not getting any answers. Nobody to this point had given any definitive diagnosis. All I knew was that I was very weak, my vision was starting to become quite blurry, my skin was darkening, and I'd started to experience ringing in my ears.

This was the point where heavy guilt began to manifest itself. I was the commander of the household—the hard worker, investor, and high-impact family man. I was home alone. My wife and kids were at work and school, respectively, and I sat in a rocking chair in our dining room, sobbing and looking out the window, feeling like I had failed everyone, especially my family. I cannot express in words the "sick-to-my-stomach feeling" created by guilt and pain commingled together. I had no idea then just how powerful thoughts are in relationship to the mechanical body response.

At this juncture, I rationalized that I would have to strike a balance between working and going back to Boston for care. After all, I did have a life, and I had obligations even if I felt like crap every day. I could take a few hours here and there for appointments and keep on working. Hopefully, the root cause of my disease could be identified and treated. At that point I said to myself: "I'll let the chips fall where they may."

I called my boss and told him I would be returning to work. He cautiously welcomed me back, and tried the tough-love approach, which was to bury me in the projects I had so enjoyed before falling to the bottom. I had been a high-level achiever before I became ill, and my boss expected me to deliver the same product I had before when life was grand. He never did fully grasp the extent of my illness during the following three years of our time together. At times, in a nice way, he inferred that my problems were completely psychological, and that "the mind drives the body." I was taken aback by his comments. I came to realize later that he was not completely incorrect. Attitude in any illness, diagnosed or undiagnosed, is key.

Going back to work was a good thing for me, because I could now focus my mind on something other than illness. It was becoming harder and harder for me to see clearly and maintain mental focus. I noticed that I was becoming very forgetful—though I had had a brain like a computer before my illness, with a razor-sharp memory. At the same time, I also knew I had to find answers to my medical issues.

I sat in my home office one day to ponder all the options. I recall mentioning to Bob Peters that I'd had severe back pains when I was in the hospital. He mentioned that he'd had a bevy of problems with his back over the years, and had found relief with an acupuncturist. I had limited knowledge of acupuncture, but was aware that Asian cultures had used the technique for centuries to cure specific ailments in the body. I called him to get the name of the practitioner he had seen.

This was my first foray into "non-traditional treatment." The "doctor" was located about 30 minutes from my home. So I made an appointment, and dragged myself to her office one bright, sunny day. I walked into a small office decorated with Japanese-style artwork and filled with soothing music. I was soon approached by a woman who greeted me, and identified herself as Dr. Jones.

I remember being a bit shocked to find out that the doctor did the intake and accounting. I distinctly remember asking Dr. Jones about her medical credentials. She indicated that the State of Rhode Island recognized acupuncturists and referred to them as "doctors." The medical questionnaire was comprehensive, and included insurance information.

After a short interview, Dr. Jones asked me to remove my clothing and dress in a gown. I did so, and she returned. She inserted razor-thin needles into the top of my head, and my arms, finger, legs, back, and feet. During the process Dr. Jones ignited some sort of incense or sweet grass. She indicated that the aroma had healing properties. I must have lain on that table for 45 minutes or more. The only thing I recall hearing was an irritating sound of a very loud vacuum cleaner in the hallway.

The doctor completed her procedure, and asked me if I wanted a follow-up appointment. I suggested that we see how it went, and said I would call her. Two days later, after severe headaches and increasing back pain, I decided to call.

"Dr. Jones, I said, "I am not feeling any better. Thank you for your care." Call me naive or foolish or badly influenced by my upbringing, but medicine as I was exposed to it consisted of men and women in white coats, with stethoscopes around their necks and pagers beeping constantly. I did not fully accept the possibilities of this type of care, and scoffed at it at first; but subconsciously, I knew that the body had the innate ability to heal itself. I have since come to understand that the field of medicine is broader that I'd thought initially, and that many non-traditional health practitioners also have a great deal to offer. (See my Resources page towards the end of this book for recommended specialists, both traditional and non-traditional healing professionals.)

I continued to search for answers. One day my father-in-law told his dentist that I was very ill. Dan the dentist is a gentle man and highly intelligent. He called me at home, and I was thrilled to hear from him. I know he sensed my fear and frustration.

Dan mentioned that he had traveled abroad and became deathly ill. He suggested I contact a local lady named Karen Williams who healed with herbs. Dan had known Karen when he fell ill, and asked her to help him. He was smart enough to know that the allopathic route could have limitations in his condition, so he sought an alternative route. According to Dan, Karen made up concoctions of herbs and tinctures for him. Dan said that in a matter of weeks, he started to feel better, and he recovered fully.

"The corkscrews unscrewed themselves," he said. "I was lucky." I thanked Dan for thinking of me and taking the time to offer his help. I called Karen, and met her at her home.

Karen was an older lady that had an appearance of a kind, gentle earthy person. Her healing room was located over a garage in her backyard. I was skeptical, but I trusted Dan.

I sat down on Karen's sofa. She offered me some tea and asked about my condition. When I started to tell her about my condition, I broke down in tears. "I NEED HELP!" I lamented.

Karen moved me into another part of her loft and had me sit in a chair. She turned a soft incandescent light into my face. She asked me to stick out my tongue. She inspected my fingernails, and looked into my eyes. You must know that I was thinking at this point: What the &#%$? Karen indicated that I should apply drops on my skin, and take oral drops which she mixed.

"Okay, I will go with it, Karen," I said. "After all, you cured Dan."

I started the regimen that day. At this point, my dining room table was filling up with all types of eye-dropper bottles. In the next four weeks, I saw Karen for two "follow-up" appointments.

I had indicated that the prescribed products did not appear to be working. She suggested I contact a Naturopathic Physician, Dr. Sara Felder, located about 30 minutes away. Reluctantly, I did. "Desperate circumstances initiate desperate actions," I thought. So I called Dr. Felder's office.

Dr. Felder was a graduate of a naturopathic college on the West Coast. She was approximately in her mid-forties, polite and firm. Of course, these docs do not take insurance, so I had to pony up. Not a problem, I had plenty of money. But please, God, stop all the paperwork. I could recite my symptoms, conditions, hospitalizations, and family history by heart. Dr. Felder's first course of treatment was to give me a shiatsu, a form of massage treatment.

Shiatsu (指圧—Japanese, from *shi*, meaning *finger*, and atsu, meaning pressure) are concepts that originated in Japan along with *Teate* (手当て, pronounced *te-a-te*). There were many hands-on therapies called *Teate* before traditional Chinese therapies, such as Acupuncture and *Tuina* (called *Anma* in Japan), were introduced to Japan around 1,000 A.D. The practice of this massage was a semi-mystical activity originally performed by women and the blind.[1]

Dr. Felder saw me five more times in the next two months. During our time together, she ordered saliva testing, stool testing, and hair samples to be sent to laboratories. According to her, these methods can be more sensitive than allopathically engineered tests for certain markers. Again, the tests showed higher levels of inflammation, heavy metals, and bacteria. On our last appointment, she prescribed a low dosage of arsenic. At that point I became very nervous. I had a background that included basic chemical engineering, and there was no way I was taking that. Seeing that I was not improving, she also suggested that I have more acupuncture. She had a partner in her practice that performed this, named Candy Smith.

I recall my first session with Candy. I walked into a small treatment room that had an assortment of human anatomy charts

---

1 From Wikipedia, the free encyclopedia at this address: http://en.wikipedia.org/wiki/Shiatsu

on the walls. Each chart had pressure points, meridian points, and various other points on the body. Impressive, I thought.

Candy held my wrists and felt my pulse. She called Dr. Felder from next door, and stared at me. Oh, my God. "Was this it for me?" I wondered. "Did they detect a fatal illness by holding my arms?" At this point I would have believed anything, and I mean anything. My double vision had progressed, and contrast sensitivity was degrading. I had started to see a "snowstorm" in my vision.

Candy Smith looked me in the eye and said: "You need to forgive yourself, George, for anything you believe you may have done wrong. Your emotions are playing a role in your illness."

"What?" I said. She told me that I needed to come to terms with the sadness in my life. "Okay," I said to myself. "One of us is crazy, and I don't think I have been diagnosed as insane yet." She then proceeded to stick the acupuncture needles in me as was done months earlier.

Can you imagine what I was feeling at that time? It all seemed so hopeless. None of the treatments I had attempted helped my situation at all. I was spending money and not getting results. I was taking time away from work and driving my family crazy talking about my illness.

After three treatments with Candy, she and I both knew that I was not getting anywhere. I begged her for guidance. She suggested that I see her mentor, who was a two-hour drive away in Western Massachusetts. What did I have to lose?

"Yes!" I said. "Please call him. I need to see him! HELP!"

CHAPTER 5

Desperation

*"Disappointment is really just a term for
our refusal to look on the bright side."*
Richelle E. Goodrich

A week or so later, I was driven by an old friend, John Casper, to this natural practitioner, named Derek Peters. We arrived early and walked around the quaint New England town together. John and I had known each other for years. He is a staunch Roman Catholic Christian who owns a supply company. He and his wife, Tamara, have hearts the size of jumbo jets. John knew that driving that distance was out of the question for me, so he took a full day out of his schedule to take me. Derek had his practice in an old office building not far from the Norman Rockwell Museum.

Again, I sat and filled out forms. This time, Derek had been briefed by Candy. We sat across from each other on a bright, sunny day in this remote part of Massachusetts, and I got right to it.

"This is what is wrong, and here are my symptoms," I said. He stared at me. I started to break down again after he told me that I had a "systemic condition" and had worsened it by putting all my energy into dwelling on it.

"Are you serious?" I said. I paid him and we left his parking lot with squealing tires. The ride home with John was very quiet. He knew that I was very depressed. We prayed together, and he asked me not to give up hope. John knew many of my concerns and issues in my life. He reassured me and told me that God was always watching me. He never wavered. Never. And to this day he is someone I can count on through thick and thin.

I took to the internet as I had so many times before to search for possible options and answers. I made a call to the infectious diseases clinic of another very high profile hospital in Boston. If I had to go to any hospital, I thought I would select one that was convenient (14 miles from my Boston office). Surprisingly, Dr. Tim Dowel, an infectious disease specialist, could see me in one week's time. Dr. Dowel was a well-established, middle-aged man, and a Harvard University Associate Professor. When we met, he showed genuine concern and interest. I knew that he would be diligent.

Dr. Dowel took the time to review my entire case and write an eight-page medical case summary. He thoughtfully reviewed my history, including all of the testing ruling out specific diseases. Like myself, he noticed my skin color changing. He also noticed that I had abnormal blood values. By this time, I had developed small spots on the base of my skull and on my knees. The spots on my skull would bleed and scab over. Dr. Dowel was perplexed. He asked if he could biopsy these mysterious bumps and lesions. I resoundingly said: "YES!" before I knew that the procedure entailed taking a circular scalpel and twisting it in those spots, taking a chunk of my flesh out for analysis and leaving a gaping hole.

Dr. Dowel was polite to me, and was clearly frustrated as our relationship progressed. He admitted to me that he was disappointed that he could not stop my suffering. In the fall of 2006, I gave him a $100 dining certificate to a Boston area restaurant with a note of thanks for his diligent efforts. He wrote me back to thank me. I suspect he had not had many of these in the course of his career. Many doctors are clearly overloaded, and are shown little formal appreciation, especially in a clinical setting.

I continued going to work, also seeing Dr. Dowel on and off for two years. At one point, we started the testing process all over again: rheumatologist, gastrointestinologist, neurologist, dermatologist, etc. All reports were sent to Dr. Dowel. I would see him, and he would continue to say: "There are abnormalities in your labs, but I cannot fit them into a clinical diagnosis." We performed a total of no less than another 78 tests over the course of my care.

In the interim, I saw Dr. Dan Devers at a neighboring medical center. He was a well-known urologist that was referred to me by a gentleman in a local country club with which I am affiliated. This man had prostate cancer, and had gone to Dr. Devers for diagnosis and treatment. By this time, I had tremendous burning pain in my groin. After a consultation, Dr. Devers suggested I return, and performed the most painful test of all, a cystoscopy. Consider yourself fortunate if you are not familiar with that procedure. I continued to press on.

During this time Dad had been giving his pal, Dr. Thomas, updates on my "medical journey." As a favor to Dad, Dr. Thomas graciously offered to call a specialist in Ohio, a very famous physician I will refer to as Dr. Magnificent or Dr. M, as I came to call him. Dr. Thomas suggested I gather my medical records and make an appointment.

Coincidentally, I had heard of Dr. M while in the office of a friend, who is also my podiatrist, and a damn good one at that, Dr. Mike King. Dr. King was originally from the Ohio area.

On a visit to his office to remove a little growth on my toe, I started talking about my medical condition. When I mentioned that I'd heard of a doctor in Ohio named Dr. M, Dr. King was astounded. He had actually attended Dr. M's lectures in medical school. Dr. King described him as a modern-day "Dr. House" with a twist: long hair in a ponytail, jeans, etc., but he was a damned genius. That truly bolstered me. So I called his clinic in Ohio, and told his staff that the "football" was coming their way. I booked an appointment and was told that as a favor to Dr. Thomas, Dr. M would review the chart and associated records in advance, thereby reducing my costs and time away from home. Two weeks before the date of my trip, I received a called directly from Dr. M.

"George, this is Dr. M. I have completely reviewed your chart. You have had exhaustive testing done in New York and Boston. Our medical facility would likely perform much of the same testing. You are welcome to come here and spend the week, and I will examine you, but honestly, in my opinion we will not be able to come up with any other answers. You have been very thorough."

All I said to myself after thanking him and hanging up the phone was, "Oh My God, I am in real trouble now!"

It was now September of 2006, one year after the initial onset of my illness. I was scheduled to go a fall safety conference in Florida for my job. One week prior, I had ceased taking the blood thinner warfarin (Coumadin). As it turned out, the day before I was to leave, I fell to the ground with an excruciating pain in my head, and experienced very blurry vision. I could barely move.

"What do I do now?" I wondered. "Do I try to go to the conference in a wheelchair? Do I mentally dismiss the crippling symptoms?" After rationalizing the options, I knew in my heart that there was no way on earth I would be able to make the trip. I got a ride to the ER, and really thought that I was going to die. I fell to pieces again, and broke down right there in the ER.

"Who can help me?" I cried. "Anyone? Please help me!" At that time my parents had not yet left for their winter stay in Florida. They made the hour and a half trip from their house to Boston to support me, and booked a room at the hotel adjoining the hospital.

The ER docs had a history of my case, since I had centered my care there. They conferred, and decided to perform a spinal tap, a procedure I had been avoiding for months at the original suggestion of Dr. Dowel. The spinal tap is a procedure where the doctor inserts a needle in the spine and extracts vials of your spinal fluid to detect a specific illness. Of course, this is a risky procedure that I would have scoffed at years before. Now I was desperate. I had to cancel my travel plans, tell my boss of my situation, call on my parents for help, and try to make sense of this to my family. I was in the ER for 24 hours for more testing and scans. The final analysis was always the same: "You have abnormal markers for inflammation, but we cannot find the cause."

Thus began a short cycle of near-insanity: of non-stop internet surfing, more doctor's appointments, and a trip to the world class facility I'd started with. I figured what the hell, I might as well! They are a top research medical facility.

I had seen specialists associated with the hospital, and maybe, just maybe, I thought, I will get that one doctor who will discover something. I recall spending 14 hours there, with much of the same result I'd had before. I sat there, hour after hour, seeing trauma patient after trauma patient go by, and I was cast aside. You have no idea how lonely and horrible a feeling it is. Doctors ran the usual blood tests, did the customary exams and released me. Same routine, same outcome.

I called and asked my close friend and buddy Chris Blake to make the hour and a half hour ride to pick me up. He was and is right there for me. We talked all the way home. "Everyone thinks I am crazy," I told him. I have known Chris for 20 years. He was the best man at my wedding, and he knows I am not crazy.

After that, I Googled unknown diseases, and found a medical doctor in Phoenix, Arizona that had a website, had published many papers, and had a long list of credentials. His name is Dr. Gene Grey.

Dr. Grey discussed hyper-coagulation in the blood during infection on his website. That truly sparked my interest, as this was one of the phenomena I was experiencing. Dr. Grey welcomed emails. So I prepared a well-thought-out discussion of my symptomology and history. Dr. Grey indicated that he thought that, based on my litany, I had an "occult Infection" of some sort, and recommended I see a local (Phoenix) nurse practitioner to reduce the "burden of pathogens" in my body. He also stated that he would not be able to see me, and he forwarded the practitioner's telephone number. Her name was Paula Williams. I called her that night. Paula listened intently to my five-minute litany, and indicated that she would be able to see me, but, as stated, Dr. Grey might not.

"I want you to immediately go somewhere for any type of oxygenation treatment before you come out. Aerobic organisms cannot survive in pure oxygen," she stated. "I know the East Coast is nowhere near as progressive as we are in this regard... try to find a hyperbaric oxygen chamber and get some time in it. Don't wait, do it now!" she emphasized.

So I started to look for resources. As luck (or so I thought it was luck) would have it, there was a hyperbaric oxygen chamber located five miles from my office complex.

I called the medical director, who was a female doctor. I explained my condition, and she scheduled me for an "interview" within the week. Her name was Grace Hole. Dr. Hole was a short, stout woman with a stern demeanor. Along with her was a kind, gentle nurse named Janice. While she was interviewing me, Janice walked in. Without a diagnosis, insurance would not pay for this.

Dr. Hole stated that the price would be $200 per session. She said, "I recommend twice a week, at 1.5 atmospheres, which is the less intrusive pressure. Each session is 90 minutes in length." Dr. Hole and Janice exchanged looks, as if to say, "We need to fill in somewhere—it might as well be him!"

At this point, the treatment looked attractive to me. It was near my office, and I could leave for two hours at lunch time to get my treatment. Whoa, not so quick, bucko.

"You need to schedule time. This chamber can accommodate up to six patients," Dr. Hole said. "Let's get you in on the schedule." I said to myself, "Self...I think you can work it in. Just think if it works! 12 minutes from the office, and just $400 per week. Well, not bad. Maybe, just maybe..." Well, you know: "This will be it...the 'silver bullet' I need to get well."

I started to read more and more about hyperbaric oxygen treatment. I knew that deep sea divers used them to compress themselves after surfacing too rapidly. I also read about a lady named Brooke Landau, a newscaster in Los Angeles. Brooke was a beautiful young graduate, just starting her broadcasting career. One day she literally could not get out of bed. Over time, her condition worsened, and became a mystery illness. Over the course of seven years, she was told she was crazy, had this or that illness, and so forth. Brooke ran the same gamut of medical insanity that I had: an endless cycle of doctors, hospitals, tests, continued decline, and sadness. Until one doctor—one brave soul—decided to inject massive doses of antibiotic directly into her heart, and administer it 24 hours per day with two months of hyperbaric therapy to force the medicine into the tissue.

Brooke's condition started to improve. Brooke has since been featured on national television to try to bring awareness to Lyme disease.

Armed with this data and information, I felt more hopeful than ever that I could edge closer to stopping my decline and hopefully use this therapy as a method to augment any other treatment. I was scheduled for my first "chamber dive" in two days.

On my first visit, I was told to go into a locker room, where I found a locker with my name on it. I changed into the all-cotton pants and cotton shirt that I found inside. Then I was shuttled to another room with shelves of boxes. Janice opened one of the boxes and pulled out a clear "space hood" with a long hose on it.

"Here, George, put this over your head. I'm going to measure your neck, and cut this rubber gasket to fit you snugly."

"What? Is this how you deliver the oxygen?"

"Yes, you each have your own spacesuit hood, and plug your hose into the port. You breathe the oxygen, and then it diffuses throughout the body under pressure. I will accompany you in now on the first dive, since you'll be alone. Now, we do have a closed circuit camera and an intercom in the chamber to monitor you. We also have a special monitor where you can watch movies. If there is more than one patient, we have a lottery to see who wins the movie selection," she joked.

Janice and I moved into an area where the chamber was located. There was a control center with all types of gauges and indicator lights, by which the operator monitored pressures and patients.

Dr. Hole sat me down to check my blood pressure and pulse. In front of me was a large circular door suspended on a blue cylinder the size of a small tunnel.

"So this is it," I said to myself. "Wow." Janice and I entered the chamber. It was well-lit, and had two bench seats opposite each other.

"Would you like a cotton blanket?" Janice asked. "It gets cold when you surface."

"No, I should be fine, thanks," I replied. I heard the door close behind us with a deep thud. Janice instructed me to take my hose and connect it to the port located in the front of the chamber. As I did, the lights dimmed slightly, and I heard a hissing noise.

"We are starting atmospheric changing," Janice said. At a certain point, she instructed me to put the clear plastic "space hood" over my head. I could not see well to begin with, and now it was impossible—everything was a blur. Janice could see that I was becoming uneasy. She sat across from me and held my hand. I started to breathe in the pure oxygen. My breathing became rapid and shallow.

Janice instructed me to try to focus on good things. "Okay, I thought...I have been ill for nearly a year and a half, my vision is blurry, and I cannot perform professionally as I did, my wife is bewildered, and I am not a fun person to be around." That was my train of thought, my "world view" at that moment, and I just could not go further into this treatment. Janice knew it, and gave the sign to Dr. Hole to stop the treatment.

I took my space hood off, and the tears were streaming down my face. Janice hugged me and reiterated that I could not lose hope, telling me of a few hard-luck cases she had seen that had turned around. She encouraged me to return in a few days as scheduled. I did, and had five more visits before leaving for Arizona, with no appreciable change in condition.

CHAPTER 6

Phoenix

*"Isn't it a bit unnerving that doctors
call what they do "practice"?"*
George Carlin

I was acquainted with Phoenix from an earlier visit. In 2004, my family and I had traveled to Phoenix when I was invited to speak at an industry conference there. We had fallen in love with the warm climate, limited insect population, and striking scenery. My mother's sister and her son (my first cousin), Drs. Thomas and Vasvi Babu met us at our resort with their two handsome sons, Nicholas and Joshua. Tom and Vasvi had started their eye-care practice in Fountain Hills, Arizona ten years earlier. After my uncle passed away, my aunt had relocated from Springfield, Illinois to the Scottsdale area.

We hung out at the pool for the afternoon, and discussed what life had been like before I became ill. These folks are woven from the same fabric as I am. They were intelligent, successful, and most importantly, kind and loving relatives. I knew that I could rely on them. I had no idea just how much I would be doing just that in the near future.

I also had one other contact in the area, my former boss, Forrest Carr. He was the Director of Safety at my firm. He and his wife Marti moved there not long before to escape the cruel New England winters and be near family. They purchased a very nice home in a remote section of town.

Forrest was a true New Englander. He still wears his Boston Red Sox and New England Patriot hat during each televised game.

Like myself, he is an engineer. Unlike myself, he does not show much emotion at all.

"Facts are facts," he once stated to me. Forrest and Marti also came to my rescue more than once.

Forrest and I spoke about the opportunities in the greater Phoenix area at that time—in 2004, before my malady. The real estate market was booming. Both he and I decided to invest in a 34-unit condominium complex in the area. Forrest and Marti had already purchased one, and planned on renting it. My wife and I bought one of the last to be built, scheduled for completion by late summer of 2005. As luck would have it, the market stayed hot, and we sold the unit in September 2005, just 12 weeks after final construction. That was great! The proceeds were, in part, used to buy a XC70 Volvo Wagon to replace our then 11-year-old Volvo. Little did I know that whatever medical bills my little business did not cover would be paid for out of that kitty. Thank you, God!

I called Dr. Grey's office in January 2007, and spoke with his assistant. She was a very direct person who indicated that it was impossible to see Dr. Grey. At this point in his life, he was not seeing anyone personally. He managed a large and growing supplement business, gave lectures at conferences for other health care practitioners, and took a lot of time off. I forwarded notes from other doctors and lab results to establish that I was not a hypochondriac with mental problems hoping to coax her (and him) into advising me on an unusual case.

A few days later, I called her back, and she indicated that in fact he would see me. I was pleased to have a personal meeting with him. At that point, the assistant asked for my credit card so Dr. Grey would not have to deal with payment. He charged $1,500 per hour.

"Okay," I thought," I can stay with my aunt, she'll feed me, and my flight was reasonable. Don't feel guilty about trying to seek answers!" Guess what, I did anyway. My thoughts of my wife and kids at home in cold New England while I was in warm Arizona added to my guilt. My family meant everything to me.

How could this be happening to me? I knew I had only spent $20,000 by this point, and I could easily make that up.

I called my Aunt, and asked if I could stay with her.

"Absolutely, no problem, sweetheart!" she answered. Good. Now I knew that I would have a family member nearby who could accommodate me. I truly never wanted to be a burden on anyone. When I arrived in Arizona, I rented a car and made a beeline to my aunt's house. I had no idea that this would be the first of nine trips out west.

Prior to my meeting with Dr. Grey, he had emailed instructions to set up an appointment with Paula Williams, as I planned on being out in Phoenix for one week. Paula was an occupational nurse who relocated to Arizona from Wisconsin. She employed a technique to reduce pathogens in the blood by using ultraviolet light and injecting pure atomic ozone—a treatment Dr. Grey swore by. So I made the appointment with Paula to coincide with his office visit.

I met Dr. Grey in a newly established office in a swank complex in Scottsdale. The new carpet smell was fresh, and ornate horse paintings were still on the floor yet to be hung. As I entered, I heard a voice in the back say to me: "I'll be right with you; go into the conference room." I sat for a few minutes before Dr. Grey appeared. He looked very healthy, and had grey hair, sparkling eyes, and large glasses that hung on his slender face.

The first words out of my mouth were, "Thank you for seeing me." Dr. Grey listened to my story and reviewed the package I had already sent him.

"Let me look at your skin." I proceeded to take my shirt off. He looked closely, then he asked to see other parts of my body. "Okay," I thought, "I am half-naked in an executive conference room in Scottsdale, Arizona. What the heck." I did everything he asked.

"You have some sort of infection," he stated. "You need to spend four hours per day in an infrared dry sauna, and you need to rotate your diet. You likely have leaky gut syndrome. That's where your intestinal tract is perforated and leaks into the tissues of the body. The body then develops allergic reactions to certain foods. I want you to purchase a host of supplements to help fight the infection, and change the 'terrain' of your body."

I listened intently and started to become overwhelmed.

"Now you have to get to Paula Williams as you indicated you would," he said. "Your blood is probably loaded with pathogens. She has a method of dealing with that."

"At this point, I will try anything, Dr. Grey," I stated. "Anything." I begged Dr. Grey to follow my case.

He looked at me quizzically, and stated point blank: "There is no way I could be your physician. I am far too busy. I have colleagues here in Arizona that can help you. Good luck," and he walked out.

Once again, I was overcome with emotion. I started to break down, sobbing uncontrollably. Mrs. Grey appeared in the doorway of the conference room. She was a beautiful older woman who looked 20 years younger than her age. She calmed me down, and took direction from her husband, who had returned to the room. He rattled off certain supplements that I needed. Both agreed that one supplement was required to improve my mood and calm my nerves. Mrs. Grey indicated that Paula Williams' techniques were excellent. She had had a horse that she loved which became very ill and was near death. Paula brought her equipment to Dr. Grey's ranch, and saved the horse's life.

"Oh, my dear Lord," I thought, "there may be hope." I left the office complex trying to take stock of my meeting.

Paula's office was in a poor section of greater Phoenix. I still have no idea how I got there, as sick and disoriented as I was. I pulled up to a western-style town that had the "tumbleweed feel." Old cars, dilapidated buildings, and farm animals were all around. I came to Paula's office, which was the size of my cubicle at work, and knocked on the door. When it opened, I saw a larger woman with salt-and-pepper hair.

"Hi, how are you?" she asked.

"I'm George Popovici."

"I know," she said. "I see you made it okay. What did Dr. Grey say?" I went into the entire story about what he thought and said as I completed the required paperwork and paid $135.00 in advance.

I sat in a chair, and Paula took my blood pressure and checked my heart with her stethoscope. Paula sensed that I had been through a lot. Next to me was a cylinder of pure oxygen; there was a box on the desk, and lots of tubing everywhere.

"How does this work?" I asked.

"The procedure requires extracting a large syringe of blood via an intravenous line, and passing it through a column of ultraviolet light, then introducing pure ozone into it," she replied. As she inserted the IV line, I could see the black blood coming out of my veins.

"See how dark your blood is?" she said. "This will turn it bright red. We go in and out three times. Now I must warn you: many of the patients I see have major reactions to this treatment. Certain pathogens may die, and the die-off causes severe illness. I call it 'race fuel' for some."

"Okay," I said, "go for it."

Paula extracted the darker blood from my vein. It passed through the UV light box and into her syringe, where it mixed with pure ozone. I found out later that ozone is atomic oxygen, and a direct biocide which kills many microbes. It's injected into tanks used by public water authorities as a precaution when transferring water from one community to another.

As Paula had promised, my blood turned bright red. She pushed it back into my body, and repeated the procedure three times. She asked me how I felt. I told her I did not feel any different than when I came. She asked me to call her the next day, and to plan on coming back in two days. So I left and headed back to my Aunt Louisa's house.

On the way I again started to question my path of treatment. Tiny offices in Arizona? Conference rooms? What the hell was I doing? Is the engineer in me driving me crazy to seek answers? I knew my condition was worsening, and I wasn't at the point where I was going to give up. No way, not yet.

Of course, out of loving concern, my aunt wanted to know everything that was going on. I was not in much of a mood to talk, and as a matter of fact, I cried most of the time. She was so consoling and loving to me. She told me that I was a good nephew, and to be grateful to God for all the good things we have. She is a woman of such strong faith, and for her age is very "with it" in terms of understanding human behavior. She's objective and wise. After all, she has three grown girls and a boy of her own (my first cousins).

My aunt knew the score, and she knew that I needed love and encouragement. Auntie and I palled around for the next day, visiting her son and his family for dinner. Tom and Vasvi are the two most laid-back people on earth. They live in a beautiful home in Scottsdale. They encouraged me to keep seeking answers and not give up.

Tom's favorite expression is, "What doesn't kill you makes you stronger." I also took the time to take Nick and Josh out for ice cream and watch their Little League baseball games. Both of them call me "UG"—a phrase coined by Tom as short for "Uncle George." Vasvi's heritage is based in India, and Tom indicated that "Uncle" in this context is a term of endearment similar to the meaning of "brother" in that culture. Not a problem for me—I loved the notion of having my two young, bright, handsome and inquisitive nephews in my presence. I had not seen them in two years, and loved the brilliance in their faces.

Paula called me later in the day. "How are you feeling?" she asked.

"No change," I reported. She said to come back at 11 a.m. the following day.

I made the 45-minute trip back out to Paula's the next day. I asked her how the hell she had ended up in this part of Arizona doing this work.

She replied, "I was a nurse in the Midwest for 30 years. My mom got ill, and we needed to move to a different climate. Arizona has one of the driest climates in the USA. So Mom and I moved out," she said. "Mom did not last long, but it gave me an excuse to relocate. I came to live here in the poor area with working folks to give back to the community. I have a small farm with animals, and I love the lifestyle. My fees are low for the type of procedure

I perform. I do see many patients with terminal illnesses that do not have insurance coverage."

Now, I thought to myself, the pieces started to fit into the puzzle. Paula was very rough in voice, but articulate in her discussion of alternative treatments.

"The body will always try to heal itself. What I do is convert the blood into a state where the microbes cannot live, so then the body returns to homeostasis. Homeostasis is the condition the body is in when all systems are balanced and normal."

I listened to Paula intently. Of course, she did not know that I had already spent a dizzying 190 hours on the internet researching unknown diseases. I already knew these principles.

I headed back to my aunt's house with the report. She was eager to hear about the different treatment and experience. I was not in the mood to really "tell all," but gave her enough information that she felt secure in my efforts to become well. The next morning I left for home.

Paula had asked me to call her upon my return home. I did, and reported to her that I did not feel or see any changes. Paula was indifferent—she indicated that at some point I might have to return. I already knew that without her saying anything. Nothing had happened, and I was very weak and ill.

Around this time, the hair on my arms started to fall out. My eyes began to turn yellow, and the ringing in my ears became more pronounced. My vision loss was progressing, and I was seeing more and more "floaters" in my visual field. Back at the house, a huge box of supplements awaited me in my dining room from Dr. Grey's office, as promised. I followed the instructions to the letter. My dining room table looked like a cross between an 11th-grade science laboratory and a pharmacy. Bottles and containers were arranged everywhere. I had to keep taking the blood thinners to keep my "infection" from intensifying my symptoms. Then came the cadre of minerals, vitamins, silver, antifungals, etc.

Taking Dr. Grey's advice, I joined a health club to sit in a sauna for long periods of time. The most I could manage without losing my mind was two hours per day.

Many naturopathic physicians believe that heating the body causes a "false fever" that kills virus and bacteria in the body. Toxins are also eliminated via the skin, which happens to be the largest organ of elimination. That was of interest to me because my skin color was getting darker by the month. I was never pale-skinned, but this was abnormal. My mother and father both commented on it several times.

So here I was, ill for over a year and a half without a definitive diagnosis, and worsening. I stuck with Dr. Grey's protocol for a few weeks, with no appreciable changes.

So the search for answers went on.

CHAPTER 7

Finally, a Diagnosis

"Man cannot discover new oceans unless
he has the courage to lose sight of the shore."
André Gide

I continued to research detoxification and neurological issues on the internet. I found the website of a doctor in Seattle, Washington who specialized in rapid detoxification via laser beam, which sounded like a possible solution. His name was Dr. Dean Kay. I called several times, and days later, I finally got an answer. Dr. Kay was very busy, and like Dr. Grey, did a lot of speaking and educating of other doctors at conferences. It would be one year before I could see him, and you guessed it: none of my treatment would be covered by medical insurance. I spoke at length with an assistant who was compassionate and understanding.

"We have calls from all over the world," the receptionist said. "Dr. Kay is well known. But I can offer an alternative. Dr. Kay had a young doctor in practice with him for three years who has now opened her own practice. Her name is Dr. Sally Dix, and she's a naturopathic physician. Dr. Dix uses many of the same diagnostic techniques that Dr. Kay does. Her office is across town, and I am certain she would have availability." I made the call right then and there, and I got an answer on the other end of the line.

I spoke with a very nice nurse name Karen. Karen was a kind lady who, like the assistant at Dr. Kay's office, was accustomed to dealing with very ill patients from all over the world. I discussed my case with her, and forwarded the football to them. One week later, I received a call from Karen.

"We can see you in three weeks, George," she said. "Plan on staying out here for one week for diagnosis and detoxification." I arranged to stay two miles away from Dr. Dix's office in an efficiency-apartment-type hotel that was inexpensive and offered the option to eat in. I had already racked up close to $60,000 in medical-related expenses. Thankfully, I had alternative sources of income to cover the costs. So the date was set: late March 2007.

As sick as I was, I decided to take vacation time, and try to downplay my illness to my employer and boss. I figured that if I died, my wife and kids would reap the full benefits of my rich life insurance policies. During this time, my boss had lightened my load somewhat. I was pleased that I had the support of many co-workers at my office. People had known me before I became ill, and they knew what I was capable of. I had won the employee recognition award in 2003 for my cutting-edge safety engineering work in introducing high visibility clothing used by the entire industry today. I felt secure in my work and my position. During the time I'd been out of the office a year earlier, I'd received many calls and emails from colleagues regarding my condition. That support was and is critical, even today.

The flight to Seattle was long and uncomfortable. Sitting next to me in the middle seat was a younger man named Frank. I eventually struck up a conversation with him, and found out he was originally from Baltimore and worked for the U.S. Army Corps of Engineers. He was going to check progress on a construction project at a Native American reservation in Washington state. He asked what I was doing. I talked about my illness, and shared the fact that I was very sad and had no idea why I was suffering as much as I had.

At one point he started to tear up.

"Oh my God," I said. "What did I say?"

"We lost my son when he was two years old," he quietly replied. "My marriage did not make it."

"Holy Moly," I thought. "I am not the only one in trouble in life. This poor man has had his world completely devastated."

I took his name and telephone number, and called him for a year after that. I now know that he was an angel sent to me to let me know that life can go on after loss.

I checked into my efficiency hotel, and decided that it might be a good idea to stock up on a few groceries for convenience and to keep costs at a minimum. By chance there was a whole foods market nearby, and I decided to walk. I huffed and puffed all the way there, but I was determined to be mobile, and to fight the good fight. The thought of being incapacitated was incomprehensible to me. After shopping, I walked back to my room and settled in for the evening's entertainment, which consisted of taking my supplements, eating fruit and almond butter, and praying.

In the morning I arrived at Dr. Dix's office, in a very upscale part of town. Her office was in a wood structure that resembled a sprawling ranch house rather than a medical complex. I walked in and was greeted by Karen.

"Hello, George!" she exclaimed. Karen was approximately 45 years old, with blond hair and a very kind, gentle way about her. She asked me to complete the stack of medical forms that is the standard fare for all practitioners.

Dr. Dix then came out to greet me. She was no more than 40 years old. Tall, with brown hair, she had a grin that made me feel very relaxed. In her cozy office, I started through the entire history of my saga. After taking notes, she explained that she performs kinesiology, which is a type of diagnostic testing that uses my muscles and her body as a guide to determine what is happening in the body.

I had read about this technique on Dr. Kay's website before deciding to make the trip to Seattle. Dr. Kay was an expert, and Dr. Dix had been his intern for three years. I lay down on a table, and Dr. Dix called nurse Karen in. Dr. Dix put her hand on my shoulder and told me to relax.

"We do all the work," she said.

These two ladies had a very detailed system that resembled an assembly line. Karen would hand Dr. Dix a vial of a certain "test standard" from a large shelf of many vials stacked in little slots. Each vial contained a pathogen, or in some cases a slide of a certain virus, bacteria, or fungal microbe. Dr. Dix put the vials or photochromatic slides (whatever the medium) on my abdomen, and then she would push against Karen's palm. I was amazed at the speed and accuracy of the whole process. If a microbe was identified, then Dr. Dix would hand it to Karen, who would isolate it in a bin. Once a group of microbes was identified, then Dr. Dix would test the entire group over again, and add or remove some of them to verify or negate.

At this point, I was not going to question this testing method. As an engineer, I had been exposed to all types of complex science and associated equipment. What I was witnessing was somewhat mystical in my mind—the idea of touching the body and using another person as an "earth ground" was totally new to me. This process went on for an hour and a half.

My bin was quite full. I tried to be patient and wait until we finished, but I had to ask questions during the process, particularly when they would glance at each other in a confirmatory manner.

"What is that? Was I positive? What is the cure for that?" I peppered them with questions.

"Well, Mr. Popovici, it looks like you have multiple co-infections. The infection is advanced," Dr. Dix told me. "I want you to spend the week with us as planned. I have a few treatments that may be helpful. Let's make up a treatment plan for you, and retest on Thursday before you leave on Friday."

"Okay," I said, "but what infections?"

She said they were both bacterial and viral. "That is why you are very weak. The infection is systemic in all organs of the body."

"Do you want to examine me?" I asked.

"Not necessary," she stated. "Our testing reveals what we need to know."

"Great," I said. "I am ready, willing, and able to do whatever you want me to do."

"Come back at 9:30 a.m. tomorrow," Nurse Karen suggested. "I am scheduling a colonic for you."

"What is that?" I asked.

"We are going to clean out your colon tomorrow. Take this pamphlet, and wear comfortable clothes—if you have sweat pants, that would be best." I decided to take a taxi back to the hotel and relax. "I was given a lot of information today," I thought to myself. "Bring it on!"

The next day I walked over to the office, huffing and puffing all the way. My muscles were killing me. My groin and legs were hurting badly. I certainly welcomed any treatments, drugs, or therapy to get me well. I was not giving up.

Dr. Dix confirmed that I had several infections in my body. At least I knew I was not a lunatic—there was a reason for my degrading condition.

As I walked into the office on morning of that second day, I met an older woman named Jane. Jane was a motherly lady with a gentle voice. She greeted me with a soft and kind "Hello."

"Have you ever had a colonic before?" she asked.

"No, I have not, but at this point," I told her, "I'm open for any treatment. Why are we doing this?"

Jane indicated that the colon is the pathway for many toxins in the body. Patients that become ill can develop autointoxication, which is the permeation of the bowel walls into the surrounding tissue. At times, parasites can live in the colon. These worms, bugs, and creatures not only cause damage, but feed off of the host.

Wowee, I thought. "Clean me out!" I exclaimed.

We walked into a wing of Dr. Dix's office that was a little out of the way and in the back. The treatment room was more like a rich library, with paintings hanging on the walls, and soft lighting.

After the colonic, I dressed and moved to the waiting area. Dr. Dix had an associate named Dr. Harvey who performed specific chiropractic manipulation. Dr. Harvey was about the same age as Dr. Dix, very pretty, and kind of a joker. She explained that the manipulation she performed stimulated the immune system. For an hour and a half, Dr. Harvey lifted, twisted, rubbed, bent, and pulled on various parts of my body. She spent much of her time turning and adjusting my head.

"I thought chiropractors deal with the spine," I said.

"That is a misconception," she replied. "We work on all areas of the body."

After my treatment, I was asked to step into the waiting area once again. There was a small boy with his mom waiting to see Dr. Dix. The boy had been diagnosed with autism. I knew that Dr. Dix used specialty supplements (primarily from Germany) to deal with specific diseases, and in the case of the boy, I learned that various binding agents would remove toxic metals from his brain.

As sick as I was, I was fascinated to learn just how the human body functions, and how it will constantly try to repair itself. Like any system, when one component has failed, it can compensate. If the failure is in a critical component, then the outcome is less likely to be favorable.

The young boy and his mom went into Dr. Dix's office. Simultaneously, I was called to the pharmacy. There I was given a "shopping bag" of all types of supplements. Nurse Karen explained each one. "This is a German formulation used for blood thinning," she told me.

It looked like cough syrup, and tasted much worse. The next was chlorella, an algae grown in Japan. It binds toxins, particularly heavy metals in the body.

"I am going to give you a prescription for a binding agent," Karen said. "This is it. It's expensive, about $400.00 per can. The local drug store has it, but I am unsure if your health insurance covers it."

"Look," I said, "if I need it, then I will buy it." She also loaded me up with a bevy of other minerals and vitamins.

I called a taxi, and went to the local pharmacy as directed. There I was told that the binding agent was not covered, and I needed to charge $400 on my credit card. This was a decision point. I was in Seattle for another three days. I thought about whether I wanted to wait, or start treating per the doctor's orders now. I opted to purchase and treat. I was going for broke, and had come too far physically and mentally to quit now. I had to get well. I needed to become myself again.

I got back into the cab, and made it into my room by late afternoon. I sat there staring at the bottles and cans of supplements. All I could dwell on at that time was that I was spending the funds I'd saved for my kids' college education, and the guilt set in. I was alone and felt it.

And indeed, I was dealing with the situation by myself. My wife had distanced herself somewhat from me emotionally by that time, saying, "When you cry wolf enough, nobody listens." My parents were supportive, but they clearly had reservations. Both my Mom and Dad could see I looked ill, but they were confused that there was no specific, detailed diagnosis. So was I.

Each day I woke up ready to head to the doctor's office. I usually ate a very light breakfast after taking the 25-some-odd pills and liquid concoctions. On the third day, I decided to walk again. The weather was balmy there, and I knew it would be good for me. Slowly I walked the two-mile trek. I was still quite weak, and had to make certain I crossed at intersections as soon as the traffic light changed or I would have been killed from speeding cars because I crossed so slowly.

Once there, I was again treated to the same therapies for the following two days. On the fourth day, which happened be Thursday, I was tested as promised. Dr. Dix and Nurse Karen repeated the same process using the muscle testing technique. I saw many of the same vials used initially being put in the "active" bin. They completed the testing, and Dr. Dix asked me to step into her office. She sat down.

"Mr. Popovici, you are a very unusual case," she told me. "You definitely have many infections in your body. There are several co-infections: bartonella and erlichia. But I am confident that what you have is Lyme disease. But the only way to truly know is to send your blood out to a laboratory called IGeneX in California. They are a 'gold-standard' laboratory that uses highly sensitive techniques to detect for borrelia."

At last I was receiving a possible diagnosis. After years of visits, stacks of medical forms filled out, insurance claims submitted, hundreds of tests undergone, supplements downed, procedures followed, thousands of miles traveled and a small fortune spent in search of the cause of my suffering, finally I was hearing a physician tell me that she believed she had identified my illness: Lyme disease. I felt immediately that I was on the right track. I was getting somewhere at long last.

When the IGeneX testing came back, it confirmed Dr. Dix's diagnosis. It showed positive bands for Lyme disease.

"How could this have been missed before in my earlier testing?" I asked. Dr. Dix had indicated in my earlier visit that the testing used in the United States would not show positive if tested in the very early stages or late stages of the disease. I asked Dr. Dix to fax me the laboratory results.

"Now I am getting somewhere!" I thought. "With copies of my test results in hand, I can tell my family I finally have a diagnosis!"

I told my wife, called my parents, and let everyone who had a concern know that I'd discovered I had Lyme disease. Sadly, by that time, my wife and my extended family had developed their own opinions as to what was wrong with me. My own father requested that I fax him the laboratory results to verify that the diagnosis was true. Most who were closely involved with me believed that my problems could be psychological. They doubted that my symptoms had an actual physical cause. As I have come to find out, this is sadly the case with many Lyme disease patients. The testing techniques are poor, and many doctors are largely ignorant of the constellation of symptoms that accompany this horrific disease. Many are even resistant to testing for and treating it.

"I know you may not want to hear this," Dr. Dix said, "but I believe your case is beyond the scope of our care. You are an advanced case, and you need advanced treatment. I am going to recommend a doctor I met at a conference in Arizona."

"Why?" I asked. "Why this doctor?"

"Well, I'll let Karen tell you. Karen, come in here please!" Dr. Dix shouted. Karen came in, and Dr. Dix instructed her to tell me about Dr. Lee Cowden.

Karen said, "I was having a internal problem in my body that Dr. Dix was having difficulty treating. I gave Dr. Dix permission to discuss my case with Dr. Cowden when we saw him at a conference. Dr. Cowden listened to Dr. Dix, then asked me to come see him right then and there. I did, and Dr. Cowden touched my knee. He told me exactly what the complication was, and what treatment would be appropriate for the issue. Dr. Cowden was right on, and I was better in days."

"Holy Smoke," I thought. "Give me my invoice and call him now," I said. "Tell him I want to see him as soon as possible." Dr. Dix knew that I was emotionally and physically drained. She agreed to call him and utilize her personal relationship with him to get me an appointment as soon as possible.

I told Dr. Dix that I had already seen Dr. Grey in Arizona. Dr. Dix knew of Dr. Grey, but had tremendous faith in Dr. Cowden based on her first-hand experience. So, on the long trip back to Rhode Island, I pondered my options. There was no doubt at this time that I had to explore all possibilities. I was fading, and everyone around me knew it. My parents were particularly concerned, and it showed. My mother was aging quickly from her worry over me. I could not just sit back and wait to deteriorate further.

Dr. Dix informed me that Dr. Cowden would take me on in short order. I called his office and spoke with his assistant, whose name was Susan. She answered a few of my questions, and set an appointment for April 21st. She also indicated that she would be faxing information about Dr. Cowden and his practice.

The following morning, I checked my facsimile machine to see a stack of information regarding Dr. Lee Cowden. Dr. Cowden was born a Texan and became a licensed medical doctor and a US board-certified cardiologist. I thought this would work out well, since I have a loving extended family that welcomes me and supports me in the area. I was very hopeful that my visit would work out better than my experience with Dr. Grey had.

But first, I learned of local options I wanted to explore as I began my battle to cure my body of Lyme disease.

Prior to my leaving for Seattle, I had made an appointment with Dr. Amiram Katz, a neurologist located in Connecticut. Dr. Katz had a good reputation for working with Lyme patients who have specific motor or sensory losses as a result of an illness. He is an associate professor at a major Ivy League university and well published. His research is used to help suffering patients around the world, many of which I have met in his waiting room. Many, I later learned, were referrals from physicians who have read Dr. Katz's work.

Upon returning from Seattle I was notified that I could be seen for a consult. As I entered Dr Katz 's waiting area I was struck by two large poster-sized photographs of happy, playful dogs. I was at first taken aback, then upon meeting Dr. Katz, I realized that his compassion extended to all forms of life, not just humans. He regularly hugs his patients and offers them hope in the form of treatment strategies coupled with just plain kindness.

Dr. Katz served as a medic in the Israeli Armed forces. Upon meeting him, you immediately sense that this tall, soft-spoken man is a highly capable professional. He is fluent in several languages and incredibly brilliant. As I scanned his office, I saw all types of awards and plaques for being voted "Best Doctor" year after year sponsored by various publications. Dr. Katz rides a motorcycle, wears jeans and draws patients' blood himself—not your typical clinician. I noticed he watched every movement I made, analyzing my gait and balance.

Seeing that I was anxious about our meeting, he took a rubber stamp from his desk, imprinted it on an ink pad and stamped a piece of note paper. He then handed it to me and said, "Do you know the angel Raphael?"

"No," I said.

"Raphael is Hebrew which means: *the God who heals*," stated Dr. Katz. With that he handed over the paper to me. I still have it in my laptop case today.

"Do not worry, Popo (the nickname he gave me right then and there), it will be alright. Believe," he said. "The mind is incredible and in order to heal you must believe and have faith that you will be well."

Wow, I thought—I am in the right place.

As he reviewed my chart, he asked me for the DVD of my MRI images. I asked him why he needed them and why he didn't simply review the hospital's radiology report.

"I want to view the images myself; it is a common practice for me."

The lights dimmed and the projector was turned on. For a moment I felt as if I was in a movie theater, about to be passed a bowl of popcorn. Dr. Katz sat behind his desk operating the computer. He reviewed slide after slide and made notes about several "white matter lesions" in my brain, using the cursor to point them out.

"I know you just returned from Seattle. I want perform specific blood tests of my own to confirm the diagnosis you have received."

With that Dr. Katz drew nearly twenty vials of blood. "We are going to send these out California, New Jersey and New York." Dr. Katz knew that I was planning to seek help from Dr. Cowden in Arizona, with whom he was familiar. "I will be back to you as soon as the results are available."

Due to Dr. Cowden's busy schedule, I was not able to get out to Arizona for four weeks, and as promised, the call came from Dr. Katz in the interim, on a Wednesday.

"As identified in Seattle, the laboratory tests confirm you are positive for various Lyme co-infections. I want to start a treatment plan for you. One specific course of treatment will include Intravenous antibiotics and immunoglobulin's (IVIG)."

At last, it was all coming together—a positive diagnosis from both mainstream and alternative physicians and a plan of treatment. All of this equated to one thing in my mind—HOPE.

"Come in this Sunday," said Dr. Katz, "and we will administer the first treatments."

As ill as I had been, I was energized to start receiving lifesaving treatments. They began with Dr. Katz, and I have continued to involve him in my case. Nothing is more important than faith and trust in your doctor. I have both in him.

With a diagnosis at last in hand, I was beginning to get the help I needed so badly. When I needed it most, I received incredible support from another special person. Ken Stann was there for me. I'd met Ken through an industry group connected with my profession and we immediately hit it off. We didn't have a direct business relationship, but it was clear that we had respect for one another and we enjoyed similar outdoor activities.

Ken owns a large optical firm in Michigan. Somehow, we happened to speak by phone on the day Dr. Katz had called me. I mentioned to Ken that I'd be receiving my first intravenous treatment on the following Sunday at Dr. Katz's office in Connecticut.

"I want to come and be with you, George. I know how long you have struggled and how lonely it is to fight without any support. I'll fly in on Saturday morning to drive you to your appointment and sit with you while you receive treatment."

The tears started to flow down my face at the sheer and utter kindness of this amazing human being who, at his own expense, wanted nothing more than to support me in my time of need.

True to his word, Ken flew in from Michigan on Saturday, rented a car and drove me two hours to my appointment. Thank God he was there because I was lightheaded and slightly nauseous after the infusion. Ken's kindness has left an indelible mark on me forever. This corporate executive with a large family, who clearly had more important matters to attend to, was there for me in my time of my need, and he continues to support my fight for health.

CHAPTER 8

Health Food Store Encounter

"A person who never made a mistake
never tried anything new."
Albert Einstein

A few days later, while I was at my local health food store, I started a conversation with one of the clerks, whose name was Mark. Mark was ill himself with diabetes. Traditional medications had not improved his condition. He knew I was also ill, and on this particular day, he mentioned a buddy of his who had been helped by a local clinic.

"Go on, Mark," I begged.

"Well, my buddy had been in a wheelchair for many years, and was told he might not walk again. He found a practitioner about 45 minutes from here who uses a cellular code technique to cure various ailments. Now the young man has started to walk again." Yes, he started to walk when he was told he probably would not.

Let me say unequivocally that the engineer George Popovici would have scoffed at this statement a few years before. Now I found myself begging him for the information. "Cellular what?" I asked. Mark said that he would call his buddy and get back to me.

I visited the health food store every day in search of Mark. Call it desperation, fear, or sheer will to live—I was truly willing to try anything.

A few days later, I received a call from Mark. He gave me the name of Alternative Healing, or AH, as most clients called it. I immediately called and asked to be seen by the owner, Gene Burns. The assistant indicted that Mr. Burns was very busy, but

I could perhaps come in midday next week. I took the appointment at AH.

The following week I left work, drove for an hour south, and reported for my appointment with Gene Burns at Alternative Healing. The place was in the corner of a strip mall on a very busy street on the west side of the state. I sat down, completed the usual forms, and waited in the small stark office, where I noticed many notarized testimonials hanging on the walls around me. I started to read statements regarding reduction in symptoms and cures due to the cellular life code system. I was excited and apprehensive all at the same time. The door opened from the small office in the rear, and the occupying client departed. Shortly thereafter, I was greeted by a burly man with blond hair, a calm voice, and a huge smile.

"I'm Gene Burns," he said. "Come on in."

I sat quietly in the small office while Mr. Burns looked over my information. "Quite impressive," he said. "Like Dr. Dix, I use muscle testing to ask your body questions."

"Okay," I said. I extended my arm to him, and he looked at me quizzically. "Don't you need to touch me?"

"No," he said, "I sit here and I can feel the energy in your presence. I twitch my index and middle finger together to obtain the information I need to determine which codes to write."

"Codes?" I asked.

"Yes, codes," he replied. "Your brain has the capacity and ability to kill any microbe that enters the body. What we do here is unlock the pathway so the brain can recognize the pathogen and destroy it. Here's how it works: you read these codes, or we say them to you. Your brain retains the information, and then you listen to this compact disc with guitar music on it."

"Guitar music?" I asked.

"Yes," Gene said. "There are frequencies that you hear disguised in the music, and that's what does the work."

"Wow," I thought, "I like this. No injections, no pills, relatively inexpensive and guess what...... he has helped many Lyme disease patients."

I told Gene that I was familiar with kinesiology via Dr. Dix, and asked him how he came to be proficient in his specialty. Gene indicated that he too had been very ill. He'd ended up on the West Coast and went to Mexico to seek answers for his life-threatening illness. Along the way, he was introduced to these "alternative" forms of healing. At that point, for whatever reason, I asked him if he believed in God.

"Yes, absolutely, and know that your eternity is assured," he said. I probably quizzed him to make sure I wouldn't be put into some sort of coma or trance that had life-altering effects. So we started, and Gene twitched away. Writing and twitching. Each time he wrote characters, they appeared as two-to-six character combinations on a "code sheet," like 6BA, 9BT, N1NA, etc. These characters had no real rhyme or reason. As bizarre as this experience was, I was bound and determined to become well, so I sat through it and attempted to believe what happening before my eyes.

After Gene completed the codes, he wrote on the bottom of the code sheet, "Thank You, God," which the client hears, reads, or both. Gene completed his work, and an assistant came into the room to read the three-page code sheet to me. At the end of this brief session, I paid my bill ($55), and left the office. I immediately inserted the compact disc into my automobile radio system to hear the music. For an hour, I listened to soft guitar music with a melody that repeated itself over and over again for that duration.

When it was finished, I called the office back as I'd been instructed, to "set" the treatment. I was told to breathe normally, hold my breath, then breathe again, and then hang up.

As ill as I was at that time, I was willing to attempt anything to gain my health back, no matter what concerns I had about the process. I wasn't gullible. I had asked the logical questions including how long the process might be. My logical, engineering mind considered the possibility that Gene could take advantage of my situation and extend the treatments for personal gain. That thought, by the way, did cross my mind several times with more than a few practitioners. (Several operate a cash business, with little tracking—and there are no insurance reimbursements or submissions for third-party payments.) So it is often a system of trust between practitioner and the patient or client.

"What about follow-up appointments?" I asked?

"Ten days should be sufficient," I was told.

"Okay," I thought, "not so bad at $250 per month."

As it turned out, Gene was an honorable man and did not prolong my visits.

"If no significant improvement is seen in three visits, then my protocol will not likely be helpful in your case," he said.

So we parted ways, in my case, with no improvement.

A few days later, I was heading out to Arizona for a second time. My cousin Tom was ready to receive me. I had the combination to the outer gate of his palatial home and a key to the front door. I was excited at this point to really "get going" after a year and a half of illness. At this point, all colors had faded away to grayish tints, and my ability to taste, smell, touch, and sleep properly were impaired.

After I arrived at my cousin's house, Nicholas, Josh and their parents came home to welcome me. Two smart-looking well-tanned young men came over to hug me. "Love is truly the great healer," I thought. We had dinner and turned in rather early because I was operating on East Coast time.

The next morning, I was awake much earlier than the rest of the household. I hadn't slept well because I was excited and hopeful about my meeting with the famous Dr. Lee Cowden. I knew in my heart that somehow he would be able to help me.

CHAPTER 9

Dr. Lee Cowden

*"For He will command His angels concerning you
to guard you in all your ways;"*
Holy Bible NIV

D r. Cowden's office was approximately 40 minutes from Scottsdale. I drove to a nondescript strip mall off of a very busy four-lane thoroughfare. As I approached the door, I noticed there were no signs except "deliveries in rear ...patient entrance." I thought this unusual, but then nothing at this point was "off the playing board" when it came to my determination to become well.

I opened the door, and was greeted by a thin, wavy-haired lady. It was Susan, Dr. Cowden's assistant. She welcomed me and gave me a hug. She asked me how my trip was, and asked me to complete the usual stack of paperwork. I sat alone in the small waiting room for nearly 45 minutes. As I waited, I noticed a framed verse from the Bible on the wall. I was comforted knowing that God was in the picture. Susan came back and stated: "Dr. Cowden does run longer than usual, and doesn't rush. Folks come here from everywhere, and often this is their last option."

"Wow!" I thought. "This must be the right place." I knew Dr. Dix would not steer me wrong.

Soon a tall, thin man with round glasses and a tweed sport coat came out to greet me.

"Welcome!" he said in a soft voice. "You ready?" I stepped into his office. I saw another Bible verse on the wall and a print of a country home with a doctor taking his bag into it.

On his desk was a laptop computer with two brass rods connected to it. In addition, many glass vials covered his desk. "Hmm," I thought, "this is unusual and perhaps very out of the ordinary, but I want whatever he is offering. I need to know what is happening to me and why."

I waited for another five minutes or so as Dr. Cowden was advising his staff on the previous patient. I could sense that his time was precious. When he returned, I handed him a few selected sheets of laboratory data and diagnosis. He glanced at them while I sat facing him on the side of his small desk. He was also glancing up at the two other assistants who were in and out of the office for a brief time.

Somehow I knew that he was a brilliant man and a healer. Then the door closed. As I looked behind me, I saw that one of them was still in the office, seated at a smaller desk with forms and pen in hand.

"May I speak with you alone for a moment, Doctor? Is that okay?"

"Of course," he answered. The assistant left for a few minutes, and I started with my history and the details surrounding my illness, which felt far too personal for me to share with others. Dr. Cowden seemed to know that I needed to establish trust. It was an emotional few minutes, and he clearly knew that I was drained and desperate to seek help. I was also beside myself with disbelief that none of the physicians I had conferred with previously could help me. Dr. Cowden's response, which resonates with me to this day was, "Forgive all the other doctors. They have done the best they knew how." He made that statement in a way that was affirming, and with the love of God flowing through him.

Dr. Cowden told me a few things before we started. He said, "Let God be the judge—do not judge yourself." Somehow, Dr. Cowden knew that I was feeling overwhelmingly guilty about the entire illness, the time away from family, and feeling like I was somehow failing them in ways I could not even begin to describe.

After calming me down, he started the procedure.

"Hold these probes in your hands. I'm starting the testing process."

He started a computer program which was detecting energy in my body. Once the process was completed, Dr. Cowden next did muscle testing using hundreds of small vials of substances. "Muscle testing is very revealing," he stated. "Toxins are stored in the body. They can also be from microbes and emotions." Focusing on the microbes, Cowden ran his fingers over the vials, and stopped occasionally. During the process, Dr. Cowden would identify specific supplements and products to be used to combat my illness in very specific intervals, such as: Magnesium Malate... one twice a day before breakfast and supper...or Samento...start with one drop before meals twice daily and build to 50 drops before meals twice daily and take for four months. At the end of the process, I had accumulated a long list of supplements and natural remedies in what seemed like sort of a Chinese checkerboard. Following the directions was a challenge in itself, and living life as a parent and provider on top of it was a real challenge.

Prior to this appointment, I had spent well over $100,000 to try to get well. The emotional toll was enormous. The feelings of guilt were totally overwhelming. Dr. Cowden knew this and took the time to talk with me about my feelings.

Three years into my journey, I had finally met a doctor who I could trust to manage my care: Lee Cowden, MD.

Dr. Cowden knew nothing about me when I first met him in his Phoenix, Arizona office. He saw me in a horrible physical and emotional state. I sat in his sparse office, upset and nearly crying. He reached over, putting his hand on my shoulder, pausing for a moment. Then he swung around and hugged me, staring directly into my eyes, and said, "You are special in God's eyes."

He asked me to picture this scene in my mind: "You are a little boy holding Jesus' hand. Both of you walk into the throne room of God. God looks at you and looks at Jesus ...He sees no difference, and he holds his arms out to you. You run to sit in God's lap, and he looks at you with nothing but love."

Dr. Cowden knew just by touching me that I had feelings of sadness and loss. In a following visit, he asked me: "What was the proudest moment you ever had with your parents?"

I responded, "When I became an Eagle Scout."

He asked me, "Remember when your mother pinned the Eagle Pin on you? And your father spoke on your behalf?"

I replied, "Yes, I do."

He looked me right in the eye and said, "That is the best they can do. They love you, but they don't know how to express it." I nearly fell off my chair. I had always longed for my parents to say how much they approved of me, but I could never express it. Those feelings were contributing to my illness. As I forgave my parents and others over time, not surprisingly I began to respond.

The first order of business on a follow-up visit was for Doc Cowden to tell me: "Forgive all the doctors you have seen, because they have done the best that they can."

These "readjustments" by Dr. Cowden proved to be life-altering and ultimately "life saving". Three and a half years before, I'd had what I perceived to be an idyllic life. Then one might say that my entire world as I pictured it had collapsed in short order. It took the compassion of this brilliant man to understand my heart and mind and to start the process of changing my thinking to allow me to start to respond to therapies. I could now start to glimpse outside the "box" that I had been stuck in.

Interestingly enough, when I look back, I do recall other doctors passing comments reinforcing the need to "stay positive" and "think good thoughts," I was sadly not open to understanding what in fact they were saying.

My local primary care physician, Dr. Marc Theroux, has the same compassion and competency as Doctor Cowden. When I visit Dr. Theroux he makes it a point to sit with me on the exam table when he reviews my chart. This gives me a tremendous sense of comfort. He completely understands how the spirit of the patient effects the outcome. He has seen this in his practice for many years. One case that I was recently made aware of was that of a teenage woman diagnosed with advanced stage breast cancer that involved most of the lymph nodes. She was treated and cured. Within a few years she married and had a family. Twenty years later, her husband abruptly left her. Within months the cancer had returned with a vengeance. This patient now requires intensive therapy and treatments. Her prognosis is guarded.

I have come to discover that you can die from a broken heart. This phenomena sometimes occurs with elderly couples also who have spent decades together. One passes away and other follows not long afterwards.

I now look back at myself in disbelief that I could not see how powerfully our emotions can effect our health. One example, personal for me, was that of Christopher Reeve, better known to most as the first modern "Superman." I met Mr. Reeve at the christening of his yacht "Sea Angel." He was a very kind to me and took the time for us to have photos together and to offer a tour of his beautiful sailboat. Not long after I met him, Mr Reeve sustained serious injuries in a horseback riding accident that left him paralyzed. His young wife Dana stood by him and encouraged him for nearly a decade in the aftermath of the tragedy. She clearly loved him deeply. Less than a year after Mr. Reeve's passing, Mrs. Reeve, a non-smoker, announced that she had lung cancer. She passed away in 2006 at the age of 44.

So at a critical turning point, I had reached a completely "different level,"—and was now able to reflect on myself in ways I had never been able to in the past: to look at myself and my situation with humility, and learn to trust my heart and gut, and to sit still and listen. It reminds me of the quote from Mother Teresa: "Prayer is not asking. Prayer is putting oneself in the hands of God, at His disposition, and listening to His voice in the depth of our hearts." That was the ONLY way I could control my negative, sad emotions, which, as I learned from others, can be fatal.

When I finally made the decision to let go of the anguish and to more consciously take charge of my wellbeing, I started to view the giant medical file that I carried around with me differently. I am still growing that file, and still fighting for my health. But I've learned through the years of ER visits and interfacing with different doctors that I can't blame anyone for my situation, including myself, or the professionals who were trained to help me but who did not understand my challenges. While at first I wondered, Why can't they fix this? I now know that things happen for a reason.

God sent Dr. Cowden as an angel into my life to reassure me that God's love is the perfect love. All humans eventually fail. We are imperfect. But God is perfect, and when we strive to seek love, kindness, respect, and humility, we are moved toward God and become like him. Only then can the healing process begin.

Note: Dr. Cowden is no longer in private practice. He devotes his time exclusively to educating physicians on chronic diseases.

Part II

Divine Order

There are difficult times in all our lives that could lead to despair and doubt. These stories helped me see that God has a plan for us. They offer us hope when we need to see past challenging times.

All in Divine Order

Did you ever lie on the grass as a youngster and stare up at the sky, and wonder how all of this came to be? I believe that all that happens here on earth is part of a divine order—thus, the popular modern expression, "Everything happens for a reason." I base my strong belief on a number of factors that point back to complete this picture.

First and probably most impressionable to me is the passage of the Bible that I have always been drawn to, Isaiah 55:8:

**"For my thoughts are not your thoughts,
neither are your ways my ways," declares the LORD.**

In that one sentence, we can know that God's plans for accomplishing his purposes are different from ours. He disappoints our hopes; foils our expectations; crosses our designs; removes our property, or our friends; and thwarts our purposes in life. He leads us on a path which we had not intended, and secures our ultimate happiness in modes which are contrary to all our designs and desires. It follows from this:

**That we should form our plans
with the thoughts of the higher purposes of God.**

**In times of trouble, turning our plans over to God is
the only way we can cope
with the unexpected and unplanned.**

There are so many times I did not understand why this or that experience happened to me. I was passed over for a job when it seemed so right for me, had a car sold right out from under me, was edged out of a ticket for a flight, and so forth. And now, I was faced with the biggest issue of all: my fight to survive and get healthy.

When we embrace the notion that everything happens for a reason, this can be tied to all life events. One such story that has deeply struck me is that of Howard Lutnick, chairman of Cantor

Fitzgerald, the investment bank and brokerage business that was housed on the 101st-105th floors of the former World Trade Center. Mr. Lutnick had taken his five-year-old son to kindergarten for his first day on September 11, 2001, and was running late to work. He arrived at the New York City tower just as the disaster was unfolding. His firm lost over 70% of its workforce. Mr. Lutnick saw to it that the company maintained its stability, and made a pledge to distribute 25 percent of the firm's profits for the next five years to the families of its 658 former Cantor Fitzgerald employees, and committed to paying for ten years of health care for them, as well.

The only way we can understand divine order is to have faith and believe.

God Moments

One of the outstanding books I have read in recent years is Lone Survivor *by Marcus Luttrell.[2] This is a brief summary of events from portions of Mr. Luttrell's book where he knew he was being protected by God.*

In 2005, Navy SEALS were dropped into the high country of northeast Afghanistan on special missions to observe and thwart Taliban fighters. On one particular mission, First Class Petty Officer Luttrell and his team of three other brave SEALS engaged 150 enemy troops in a vicious mountaintop firefight after their whereabouts were given away by tribal local goat herders who stumbled across them.

Although the SEALS were effective, they could not stop the sheer numbers of enemy soldiers from advancing, so the team had to fall back, or in Marcus Luttrell's words, "fall off" the backside of the mountain. With no other options, they did just that, spinning out of control and careening at high speeds down the mountain, with all equipment ripped away from their bodies as they fell 200-300 yards straight down into dirt and boulders.

Petty Officer Luttrell makes this statement regarding his situation at that moment in his book:

"I rocketed up the lip of that back slope making about eighty knots, on my back, feet first. In the air I made two complete back-flips and I landed on my feet again feet first, on my back, still coming down the face of that cliff like a howitzer shell. And at that moment I knew there was a God.

"First of all, I appeared not to be dead, which was right up there with Jesus walking on the water. But even more amazing was I could see my rifle not two feet from my right hand, as if God himself had reached down to me and given me hope. Marcus, I heard Him say, you're going to need this. At least, I think I heard him. In fact, I swear to God I heard him. Because this was

---

2   *Lone Survivor,* by Marcus Luttrell is published by Little, Brown and Company

a miracle, no doubt in my mind. And I had not even had time to say my prayers."

I read that book four years ago, and never forgot the impact of Petty Officer Luttrell's statement regarding his "God Moment." I believe that PO Luttrell was spared on that mission to come back and tell his story of faith, courage, bravery, and the ultimate sacrifice of those SEALS on that day.

God Has a Plan

I have been a fan of Dr. Wayne Dyer for many years. I had the opportunity to hear him speak in person in Boston, Massachusetts a few years ago. I was particularly struck when he spoke of one life-altering event that he wrote about in detail in his book, You'll See It When You Believe It.[3] *I strongly recommend that you look into the many good works of Dr. Wayne Dyer. A brief summary of Dr. Dyer's experience follows:*

Dr. Dyer was born in 1940, the youngest of three boys all under the age of four, to a father whom he did not know. His father abandoned his family when Dr. Dyer was two years of age. His mother could not provide for him, so he was relegated to foster homes, with his mother visiting when possible. Dr. Dyer developed anger toward his father, and ultimately hatred. Eventually, that anger turned into curiosity, and he became fixated with the idea of wanting to meet his father.

Over time, Dr. Dyer became obsessed with finding his father, and made contact with his father's side of the family in his attempts to locate him. They were of little assistance, because they feared that Dr. Dyer's mother would arrest his father for lack of support. He traveled to meet ex-wives in distant cities, and made phone calls, but to no avail. During his college years in New York City, his dream about finding his father continued to intensify, and he would awaken in fits of anger.

In 1974, Dr. Dyer accepted an assignment in Columbus, Mississippi. He telephoned a cousin who had called four years earlier with a reported sighting of his father in an infirmary in New Orleans. At the time, Dr. Dyer could not leave his family to pursue his nightmare. Upon arriving in Columbus, Dr. Dyer called the Infirmary, and learned that his father had died ten years earlier, with the body being shipped to Biloxi, some 200 miles away from Columbus. Having an extreme desire to "close out" and resolve

---

3   *You'll See It When You Believe It: The Way to Personal Transformation*, by Wayne W. Dyer is published by William Morrow Paperbacks

this entire matter, he rented a brand-new car to make the drive to speak with his father's friends to discern whether Dr. Dyer or his family had ever been mentioned.

Now here is where I believe God stepped in to bring Dr. Dyer to a higher level of awareness. When he went to rent the car (which had less than one mile on the odometer), he noticed that the lap belt was missing. So he took out the entire bench seat, and saw that the belt was taped to the floorboard and the buckle wrapped in plastic, secured by a rubber banding. As he lifted the belt, he tore off the plastic cover to expose the buckle. In the plastic was a business card tucked inside which read, "Candlelight Inn, Biloxi, Mississippi," and had a series of arrows leading to the establishment. Dr. Dyer thought it was very odd to find a business card in a plastic wrapper in a brand-new car, but without hesitation, he tucked it in his pocket and headed to his destination.

When he arrived on the outskirts of Biloxi late on a Friday afternoon, he stopped at a gas station to call cemeteries. There were three listed. The first line was busy, the second had no answer, and the third (and least impressive listing) was answered by an elderly man. When Dr. Dyer inquired regarding his father, the voice on the other end asked him to wait. A full 10 minutes went by, and just as he was about to hang up, the voice came back on the phone.

"Yes, your father is buried here. We are located across from the Candlelight Inn, just three blocks away. Come now, and just put up the chain when you leave." Dr. Dyer stood there shivering as he looked at the business card he'd found in the brand-new car parked just a few feet away from him.

Dr. Dyer went to his father's grave, and experienced an overwhelming calm after two and a half hours of releasing him and forgiving him. He stood by his father's gravestone, saying, "I send you love." All kinds of miracles happened to Dr. Dyer after that. He is now a world-renowned author and speaker, and has helped millions of people understand that everything is a part of divine order, and that God has a plan.

Part III

Miracles

The sole surviving artifact after fire took 100 homes
in Long Island during Hurricane Sandy
Photo with permission jameseroche.com

These are the stories that were told to me
over the course of my healing – the stories
that Maureen Hancock told me people
would bring to me. In my mind, these
miracles show the power of God over and
over again, and I am pleased to share them
with you.

A Medical Miracle

Pastor Jordan S.C. Jacobson is the pastor of Friends Church in Portsmouth, RI. I was introduced to the pastor by a mutual acquaintance who began attending the church when her marriage of 30 years ended. The following four stories are the result of hours of collaboration with the pastor. The first is Rachel's story, as told by her father, Pastor Jordan:

We were living in Virginia in 1992. I was a Physician Assistant in medical training. At the time, we were living in Virginia and I was working at large area Hospital. I was an associate pastor at that time.

My daughter Rachel was ten and a half years old, and had been complaining of pain in her back for weeks. We took her to the family doctor, who thought she had a back strain because she was an active girl. Sometime before, she had taken a very bad fall, and cut her chin. When we visited the doctor, Rachel explained that her legs had quit working, and that caused her to fall. And over time, the symptoms had subsided.

It was Martin Luther King, Jr. Day in 1992. The family had planned a day together, and I told Rachel to get up. She indicated that her legs would not work again. I told my wife, Judy, to keep Rachel distracted while I performed basic nerve testing in her bedroom. When I realized there were no reflexes, I called our family doctor. Since it was a holiday, the offices were closed, but due to the relationship we had, the doctor agreed to open his office to see us.

We arrived at the office, and after a cursory exam by the physician, he determined that Rachel needed to go the hospital. He said he would prearrange for a neurologist to meet us there. I recall vividly that I had to carry Rachel into the hospital because she was not able to walk. And I also clearly remember that before reaching the entrance, I turned to Judy and said to her, "We're all going in, but we're not all coming out." In my heart, I knew that there was something very serious happening to my little girl.

The neurologist again performed a basic evaluation on Rachel. He ordered immediate MRI and CT scans. During the course of the tests, the MRI was repeated three times, which was highly unusual, and this gave me a very sinking feeling. When the neurologist called for a consult with our family, I knew this was serious. He informed us that Rachel had a tumor which was wrapped around her diaphragm and lung, had advanced to her ribcage, and then had gone to her spine, where it had displaced three vertebrate and attached itself to the spinal cord. The neurologist indicated that emergency surgery was the only option due to the possibility of paralysis as a result of the tumor on the diaphragm. If it continued to grow, Rachel would not be able to breathe. He further explained that the invasion of the tumor into the spinal cord was what had caused Rachel's inability to walk. It was stated clearly that there were no guarantees that Rachel would regain any mobility or ability to walk again, even with a surgical procedure, as the spinal cord damage was difficult to assess.

Due to my working relationship with many reputable physicians and surgeons, I was able to select the surgeons who would perform the operation. The procedure was somewhat complex, and required two specialties: a thoracic surgeon to deal with the diaphragm, lung, and ribcage, and a neurologist to address the spinal cord.

As it happened, the first surgeon selected was Dr. Walters. I knew of Dr. Walters because his parents lived across the street from Judy's mom and dad. So his talent was well-known, and he was familiar to the family. The second surgeon selected was Dr. Jim Peters. Dr. Peters was a well-known neurosurgeon who devotes his time to medical missions in third-world countries, performing difficult procedures on children specifically.

All this happened within a 72-hour time period, and events were moving rapidly because Rachel's life was in the balance. The day of the surgery, it was decided that the thoracic surgeon would lead in this procedure. After five and a half hours, he came out to speak with Judy and myself to indicate that he had completed his procedure and had turned Rachel over to Dr. Peters to complete the process. At that time, he stated that he had removed the tumor from her diaphragm, and had to remove a section of her lung as well. As he had attempted to remove the tumor from the ribcage, three of her ribs literally crumbled in his hands.

Now it was Dr. Peters' turn. He emerged after an additional five hours. I knew him personally. As a result, I asked him directly, "What are we dealing with?"

"I really don't know, and won't until I get the pathology reports," he said. I stared him right in the eye and said, "Jerry, I'm not asking you to name it. You have done many of these surgeries—please give me an idea of what we're looking at."

He responded, "I've never seen a tumor such as this. It was definitely aggressive and malignant, and I cannot comment further without scientific evaluation." After the procedure, we went to recovery to see our little girl. Unknowingly, we walked past her twice, and then inquired where Rachel was. She was grossly disfigured, and unrecognizable to us. Chest tubes protruded from her little body. We sat with her until Rachel was transferred to the intensive care unit, where she remained for several days before being moved again to the children's oncology unit.

The tumor was highly unusual, and had to be sent to Sloan Kettering in New York, Albert Einstein in the Bronx, New York, Duke University in North Carolina, the Mayo Clinic in Minnesota, Dana Farber in Boston, and the National Institute of Health Science for identification. A few days later, I was at the hospital with Rachel, and Judy was home with her siblings. I called for my own Pastor, Frank Carter, to come to be with us. Dr. Jane Burton, a pediatric oncology physician, approached Rachel's room with Pastor Frank and I present. She motioned me into the busy hallway, and stood before me, proceeding to take her fingers and hold the digits out and enumerate her points by touching each one as she spoke.

"Your daughter has an ugly, virulent form of cancer from which there is no recovery. I suggest you take whatever solace you can find from whatever source you believe in, and make the appropriate arrangements. Your daughter will not survive."

A 100-pound sledgehammer was dropped on my heart and head. Dr. Burton further informed me that to date, only six known cases of this type of cancer had been diagnosed in the USA. All cases were females, and none survived. The cancer is called mesenchimalchondrosarcoma.

I immediately called Judy with this horrifically sad news. Upon answering, this anxious mother asked me "Was there any word?" and I recall telling her yes. As she pressed me for more information, I responded by saying, "We began our life together at the altar, and have brought all of our children to the altar and had them dedicated to God. I will meet you at the altar, and tell you the rest. Pastor Frank will come to pick you up."

Judy arrived at our church, Portsmouth Friends Church. I told Judy word for word what Dr. Burton had indicated. We hugged each other and Pastor Frank, and prayed and cried. Immediately following, a decision had to be made whether to commit Rachel to radiation and chemotherapy treatments. Dr. Burton was convinced it would not change the prognosis of certain death.

Judy and I had been married in Virginia Beach (close to our home) some 10 years earlier, and I had always had a connection to Pastor John Geminez. My relationship with him was unusual in that our paths crossed multiple times in significant ways. Pastor Geminez was also the man who dedicated Rachel when she was born. Judy and I decided to confer with Pastor Geminez to help us with this very difficult and awesome decision laid before us. We were torn, because in our hearts we did not want to give up; however, the doctors felt it was in fact hopeless.

It is difficult for a parent to give up on their child, no matter the facts or the odds. Our church was small when we married, and had exploded into a mega-church. Pastor Geminez was now surrounded by a large staff that orchestrated his schedule and those who have access him. I needed his advice and counsel to help Judy and I make this terrible decision regarding our little girl. I trusted Pastor Geminez, and we needed him. So I decided, after many unsuccessful attempts to reach him, to drive to the church one day and sit on the step which he had to use to gain entrance into the church. He arrived, we met, and we went into his office.

I told him the challenge that we faced, and unexpectedly Pastor Geminez reached over to his desk and turned a picture frame towards me which contained a photograph of a little baby. I assumed it was his daughter Robin, but upon observance I realized it was a picture of my Rachel! It was sitting on his desk 10 years later. I was astounded. After the hundreds of baptisms he had performed, my daughter's photo adorned his desk!

Pastor Geminez looked at me and said, "There is a scripture that says, 'Having done all, stand.'" Then he stopped speaking.

I asked him, "What does that mean?"

He stated, "You must do all you can do to stand not only medically but spiritually." When I left Pastor Geminez, I had clarity, and I knew that we had to commit to the regimen regardless of the prognosis.

I returned home, and shared the discussion with my wife. Judy paused, knowing well what a commitment to treatment would entail. I reengaged Dr. Burton to discuss how the treatment would proceed, and she indicated that the protocol would entail a 24-month period of chemo and radiation. With that she restated that there were no guarantees, and that following this path might only prolong the inevitable. And that at any point during the process, our little girl could succumb.

Rachel was still hospitalized at this point in a private room. Dr. Burton indicated that a multiplicity of chemo drugs would be administered, some so toxic that there would likely be damaging effects to the heart and kidneys, so that in going forward Rachel would also likely have complications with her urinary system. And so we began the process.

As you can imagine, this event turned our life upside down, both emotionally and physically. We had to split our time: Judy stayed with Rachel during the day while her siblings were in school, and I would leave work and take over at her bedside while Judy attended to the other children at home.

Rachel had stabilized from the radical surgery, but continued to remain hospitalized so that the aggressive regimen of cancer-fighting drugs could be administered. This continued for one week, and then she was discharged and allowed to go home.

While Rachel was at home, I was given the responsibility to administer injections daily to keep her blood count at an acceptable level, as well as take care of her central medication line. During the course of that time, Rachel would eventually "bottom out" and have to be re-admitted to the hospital, since her white blood count was depleted.

This process continued in a cycle: Rachel would spend 10-12 days in the hospital, return home again for 3-4 days, and then start the regimen all over again. This cycle repeated itself for nearly two years.

One can't imagine the changes this caused in our lives. We could not expose our little daughter to any situation that might compromise her or cause further issues with her immune system. As a result, she was semi-isolated from the general population and most activities.

We had been warned about exposure to cold. It rarely snows in Virginia Beach, but this winter it had snowed on and off, which was unusual. After seeing her brothers having fun, Rachel wanted to play. I recall that she had asked to go outside several times, and each time Judy explained to her why she could not. Judy had to watch her little girl stare though a window as her brothers had fun in the snow. Eventually, Judy went back to Rachel's room with her coat, hat, and gloves, and having dressed her warmly, told her she could go out for 10 minutes. As she watched her little girl go through the door, Judy started to cry.

I asked her, "Why are you doing this?"

She replied, "If Dr. Burton is correct, and she is going to die, then I don't want to be the one to take this away from her." I knew then that it might be impossible for anyone who is not faced with a challenge such as this to understand a mother's heart and how it breaks for her child.

As spring approached, we were contacted by the Make-a-Wish Foundation, a well-known organization that offers positive experiences for terminally ill children and their families. When Rachel was asked what her wishes were, she replied, "A cruise on the Disney Big Red Boat."Of course much concern surrounded this plan, as Rachel would be out of the country, away from her physicians, exposed to many people, and confined on a ship. But we wanted to make her dream come true.

Once the doctors had approved of the trip, preparations began, which included staying three days and three nights in DisneyWorld, then boarding the ship for a five-day trip to the Bahamas. We had to receive special clearance to carry medical devices, which included syringes and a portable IV pump. We flew down to Orlando, and upon our arrival, Rachel crashed. She was taken by ambulance to Arnold Palmer Children's Hospital, where the doctors immediately conferenced back to Virginia for medical direction. Rachel remained in Arnold Palmer Hospital, receiving blood transfusions and other medical attention to stabilize her until the time we were to board the ship. The rest of the family went on to DisneyWorld, and Judy and I stayed back at the hospital.

Rachel had stabilized, but questions were raised regarding her ability to continue the trip in her weakened state. I specifically recall having a conversation with the Virginia medical team, in which they indicated that it was solely our decision to continue or abandon the trip. If we returned to Virginia, Rachel could still fail; if we continued on the trip, we might face the same outcome. The doctors stated that they would fly the necessary blood as well as additional medications to us if we chose to continue on the cruise.

Once again, the heartbreaking decision had to be made: continue on the trip, or return home. Judy and I spent much time praying, and decided that since there were no guarantees either way, we would spend that time doing what our little daughter wanted. Amazingly, upon boarding the ship and getting settled, Rachel began to recover immediately!—so much so that we were able to have dinner in the main dining room with all the other guests. What a moment! We knew then that we had made the right decision. And for the remainder of the cruise, Rachel grew stronger and had an enjoyable experience.

We were together as a family, and my oldest son (also named Jordan) took this opportunity to announce his engagement to my future daughter-in-law. Life seemed semi-normal, and we were happy to be together and seeing our daughter happy. We returned from the cruise with a renewed outlook on the future.

My son was cognizant of the fine thread on which his sister's life balanced, and wanting to ensure that Rachel was a part of his wedding, proceeded to move quickly with his wedding plans. We made arrangements to have Pastor Frank perform the ceremony in the following months. It was typical wedding planning, but in an accelerated fashion so as to "put at ease" my son and his concern for his sister's inclusion in the event. Invitations were sent, dresses were selected, and the cake design was discussed.

Approximately three months later, the day of the wedding arrived, and Rachel, wearing her tiny wig, was dressed as one of the bridesmaids. She was standing at the same altar where I had broken the news of her serious life-threatening illness to her mother.

During the service, Pastor Frank was offering a prayer prior to the pronouncement of declaring my son and his fiancée man and wife when I heard a rustling noise. I raised my head from prayer in time to see my little Rachel slump to the floor. Before I could leave my seat, one of the elders from the church who had witnessed the event scooped her up into his arms and brought her to another room in the church. The wedding continued as Judy and I rushed Rachel back to the hospital. Rachel confessed to us that day that she had felt ill all week, but was determined to be at the wedding, and so she kept her condition a secret. What a trooper!

Once again, we started the cycle of stabilization at the hospital and then returning home. The process continued for another 8-9 months. In that time, we rode the roller coaster of highs and lows, both medically and emotionally. As you can imagine, other families we met at the hospital experienced the same trauma, and it was expressed in many ways: loss, sadness, and despair, which without faith takes a huge toll on everyone involved. You see, I firmly believe that it was our faith in God that allowed us to press on with the seemingly impossible.

At the close of the 20-month cycle, Dr. Burton indicated that it would be prudent to discontinue the treatments due to the fact that toxic levels of the chemotherapy drugs were causing more harm than good.

So on the last day at the hospital, the doctors removed the central medication line, which remained in perfect condition, as I had personally cared for it during the entire treatment period. The medical team had done all they could, and they wished us well.

Over time, Rachel's white blood cell counts maintained normal levels. She continued to take oral medications, and was monitored by medical doctors. And so began the next part of our journey to reclaim a life that seemingly had no hope for survival.

Rachel started to recover slowly. Since the cancer had affected her spinal cord, it also impacted her nervous system, and caused some permanent damage, so her ability to walk was limited. Each doctor's visit, however, continued to confirm that the cancer had not re-established itself in her fragile body.

Rachel returned to school, but was not able to participate completely at first due to her physical restrictions. Day after day, month after month she continued to improve and develop a sense of stability in her health. Her functions began to return, and she started to act like a semi-normal teenager (if there is such a thing). We breathed a sigh of relief, knowing that the worst was behind us. This is amazing in itself for someone who was given up for lost.

With all of the life changes that had taken place, it was now time for one more to occur.

Early on, I had attended seminary with the intention of becoming a full-time Pastor. Since I had a family, I had decided to take a position at the hospital to support my family while continuing my studies. I completed my seminary training, and at that time there were no local churches that could support a full-time pastor with a family who had our financial needs. So I continued at the hospital, and advanced my medical education and training. But my first calling was full-time ministry.

It was now 1999, and Rachel's siblings were no longer living at home. Rachel was approaching her senior year in high school, so Judy and I decided that we should seek a full-time ministry. As it happened, we moved from Portsmouth, Virginia to Portsmouth, Rhode Island as I accepted a position as Pastor of Portsmouth Friends Church. Rachel enrolled in the local high school, where she was the only student allowed to use an elevator when no wheelchair was required.

As we settled in, and were greeted by the community, I sought to find a good local family doctor. I took it upon myself to walk over to the fire station to ask the guys who they might recommend. One name popped up: Doc (who George Popovici had originally seen years before), who practiced down the road. I made an appointment for an office visit, and met him a short time later. As we sat down, he noticed I was from Portsmouth, Virginia. He commented that he had recently read an article in a medical journal about a child from that area who had been diagnosed with a rare cancer who had in fact survived.

I said, "Would you like to meet her?"

He asked, "Do you know her?"

I replied, "That is my daughter, Rachel." Needless to say, he was shocked. I look back at that encounter, and know that everything happens for a reason, and that all we have been through with this miracle child was for a reason.

Eight years after she was diagnosed, we watched our daughter cross the stage to accept her high school diploma. Four years after that, we watched her graduate from college. I had the privilege to perform the wedding service for my little girl some six years after that. And I have become a recent grandfather.

God has a plan for all of us. Which brings me to what Jesus said: "With man it is impossible...but with God all things are possible."

God gave us our daughter back. Rachel's outcome was good, though some are not, but you can never give up hope.

It's Going to Be OK

The following stories are also contributions by Pastor Jordan Jacobson:

It was Christmas of 2006, a time of miracles and gift-giving, a time when we're reminded of God's gift of Jesus into the world, and this particular year, in a quiet way the gift of a woman named Becky came into our lives.

My son Jordan's first marriage had ended years before. Jordan had never returned to dating again, because he had two children from his first wife, and was focusing his attention on their needs and being an attentive dad.

Much like the world not expecting the gift of Jesus, Jordan was not expecting to meet a woman with whom he worked who would change his life dramatically. What is interesting about this is that Jordan became very interested in her, and Becky was not particularly interested in him. Jordan spent many hours on the telephone with Becky expressing his deep inner feelings about his life and faith.

Judy and I knew of Jordan's interest in Becky, and were eventually introduced to her. Jordan brought her to the house, where we met a pleasant young lady who was kind and respectful. As parents, we had hope that Jordan would always focus on the children and keep an open mind.

As time passed, it became apparent that Jordan and Becky were becoming involved. In those winter months, Jordan had a close call with a motor vehicle accident, and he wasn't sure whether he was going to come out of it alive or not. But through that ordeal, his only concern was for Becky. Shortly afterwards, Jordan asked Becky to marry him.

In June 2007, I joined my son and Becky in wedlock. They settled into the marriage routine rather uneventfully. Both of them continued their employment at the same firm. Life was good, until they hit the first speed bump. Both Jordan and Becky were laid off within two weeks of one another. Ironically, in the search to seek new employment, they were both were hired into a new firm together! Amazing! So, once again, they were in each other's company in a working environment.

Becky had decided to go back to school to pursue an advanced degree, and was accepted into the program she chose, so everything seemed to be falling into place. Unexpectedly, over a Sunday dinner, they informed us that Becky was pregnant.

Being parents ourselves, Judy and I were both surprised and concerned, knowing the struggles of balancing new jobs, parenting, and school. All seemed well, and then on November 26th, the day before Thanksgiving, their son Benjamin was born. Judy and I took the Thanksgiving meal to Becky in the hospital, with a large serving of banana pudding.

Jordan met us at the entrance to the room, and commented to his mother, "Mom, you know I don't care for banana pudding," to which she replied, "Sorry honey, it's not for you. It's for Becky." At that moment, as we entered, Becky handed Benjamin to Judy, and said, "Here he is...he is yours." Judy was beaming. Becky's statement has incredible significance, which I will explain shortly.

Becky was discharged with her new bundle of joy, and after the appropriate leave, resumed her position at work. Thus began the balancing act of life with a newborn and juggling schoolwork. Judy and I saw them every week, and shared experiences and discussed issues regularly. Occasionally, Becky would complain of pain in one of her breasts. An appointment was made for an office visit with a local doctor. Becky explained that she was a new mother, and detailed her breastfeeding activities, at which point the doctor was convinced it was nothing more than a blocked milk duct, and would likely resolve on its own.

As a medical professional, I asked Becky what had transpired at the doctor's office, and she detailed the conversation. Under normal circumstances, I would have questioned why diagnostic testing was not performed, but we were in the thick of planning Rachel's wedding, so I admit I was distracted.

All our focus was on Rachel at this time. Becky was a bridesmaid, and completely enjoyed all the family festivities with no apparent outstanding issues. Towards the end of June, Becky began to complain again, this time of severe headaches and occasional loss of equilibrium. I recall being at Rachel's house on the Fourth of July, and Becky, Jordan, and baby Benjamin were there as well. We decided after viewing the oldest and largest Fourth of July parade in the nation that we would stroll through the town to enjoy the sight and fellowship of one another. During that walk, Judy, Rachel, and I noticed that Becky had some difficulty walking. Often she would lose her footing and stumble. I was concerned, and suggested that she have a follow-up appointment with her doctor ASAP.

It was a few days later that Jordan and Becky to inform us that the doctors had performed tests, and determined that Becky had cancer. At that point, all the memories of Rachel's ordeal came flooding back. We were in shock.

I knew that time was of the essence, and I immediately instructed Becky to get to the Dana Farber Cancer Center in Boston. Dana Farber is a world-class facility. You may recall from Rachel's story that doctors there had assisted in identifying Rachel's cancer, and also in determining the treatment protocol. Thankfully, Becky was seen at Dana Farber within days of the initial diagnosis.

Once again, Jordan and Becky came to our house to discuss what had transpired. The doctors had informed them that Becky's malady was "bad."

I immediately cut Jordan off, and said, "We have been down this road with your sister, and we can get through this."

Becky then turned to me and said, "But Dad, you don't understand—the doctors told me this was terminal."

I replied, "I don't care. We've heard that before, and I'm not giving up." Over the next several weeks, Becky returned to Dana Farber to have more tests performed.

Becky became quiet about her condition at this point. Jordan was understandably very unsettled. After all, he was a newlywed with a newborn baby. It tortured Jordan to know that the doctors had not yet formulated a treatment protocol for the love of his life. He was struggling with this, and it was a very difficult time for all of us, but especially him.

As was their routine, Becky and Jordan would come to my church on Sundays. Sunday Sept 13th, 2008 was particularly significant, because it was Jordan's birthday. We had planned to go out to dinner as a family after the service. As we crossed the parking area from the church to our home, Becky indicated that she was not feeling well at all. She had a severe headache and nausea. Being the person that she was, Becky encouraged us to go ahead and have dinner and leave her at the house. Of course we as a group would have none of that, particularly Jordan, but Becky insisted.

So we decided to go to a local restaurant for dinner. I can categorically state that there was little dinner conversation. We hurriedly ate our meals so we could return back to Becky's side. Upon arriving at the house, we found Becky reclined in my easy chair. Her skin color was pale white. In a weak voice, she said that it felt like her head was going to explode. I had Jordan call Dana Farber immediately, and the doctors admitted Becky on the spot.

Once in the hospital, doctors again performed more tests, and determined that the cancer had invaded Becky's brain, thus causing the headaches. Within hours, Becky was taken to the operating room, where surgeons performed emergency surgery to remove as much of the masses as possible for the purpose of affording Becky some relief.

Once in recovery, we had the ability to confer with the medical team. Doctors said that it was likely that these procedures would not save Becky's life, but rather prolong it. We felt like we were reliving the past all over again.

A few days after the surgery, Becky started to experience abdominal pains. Further tests revealed that masses were present all throughout her intestinal tract. Although I don't know for certain, I believe the doctors at this time were evaluating the risks and benefits of further surgery. Approximately a week later, her pain became so intense that surgery was indeed scheduled.

During the procedure, it was discovered by the medical team that the cancer had perforated parts of Becky's intestines, and bile and fecal matter had escaped into the abdominal cavity. Sepsis was a great threat at this point. Surgeons removed intestinal tissue that was too damaged to repair. Other areas of the intestinal tract were repaired to the best of their ability. Then Becky's entire abdomen and GI tract was washed to prevent infection. The surgeons created a colostomy for Becky because so much of her bowel was unable to be repaired. She also had to be put on a ventilator to assist with her breathing.

Becky was moved to recovery yet again, and when the medical team requested to meet with Jordan, he called me at the house and asked if I would come to be with him during this meeting. Rachel's husband Rob and I went to Boston that day to meet Jordan. When we arrived, he came down to the lobby to meet us. The three of us went outside, where Jordan informed us that the doctors were assembling the remainder of the medical team to share their expertise. However, the oncologist's report trumped all the others in his assessment that Becky was dying, and that there was truly nothing that could be done to save her at this point.

The three of us went back upstairs, and were taken into a conference room. Jordan sat with Rob on one side and me on the other. A small group of people began to gather: a social worker, patient advocate, oncologist, surgeons both neurological and thoracic, and the lead nurse assigned to Becky. Each of these professionals summarily came to a similar conclusion as each detailed their medical observations and results.

At the conclusion of the assessments, Jordan asked the doctors if I as his father could ask a few questions. My medical training kicked in, and I started to ask pointed technical questions regarding Becky's case. During the exchanges, I sensed the doctors becoming more guarded with their responses.

Toward the end of the session, I began to realize that the doctors had come to their own conclusions regarding Becky's condition. Specifically, they were seeking to have Jordan make the decision to remove her from the ventilator, make her comfortable, and allow her to pass away.

To my utter amazement, I watched as my son stood up from his seat and began to address the group. We watched tears stream down his face as he expressed his deep appreciation to each of the medical professionals in that room. He then spoke of his concern for his wife's condition, and in a kind but authoritative voice, said, "I want everything to be done that can be done until there is nothing more that we can do. My wife is alive, and I intend for her to stay that way as long as it is possible." I have had many occasions to be proud of my son during his life, but none of them compared to my deep sense of awe in this very moment. The meeting was concluded by presenting a 48-hour ultimatum to Jordan regarding her status with the ventilator.

Within the next few days, Becky became conscious and started to breathe on her own. She wanted the breathing tube removed. Jordan called us, and indicated that he wanted us there for this event. Judy and I responded. Jordan came out of intensive care to meet us.

As we entered the ICU cubicle, Becky was in a semi-inclined position in her hospital bed, and she looked at all of us. Just then she said, "Come here, you gorgeous hunk of man!" I thought she was talking to her husband, and I looked over my shoulder. Nobody was there. She was talking to me.

I walked to her bed, and she reached up for me and hugged me. She said, "I have something to tell you. Nobody will understand what I am about to say, but you will." And then she began to tell me of her encounter with the Lord.

These were her words: "Dad, I just saw Jesus, and it was so awesome. It's just like you said at church. I was in this great light, and yet the light was in me as much as I was in it. That's when I realized all that you had said was real. He was in me and I was in him."

Judy was on the other side of the bed, listening, and addressed Becky intently: "What did he look like?

I observed Becky's face change, and her whole appearance took on a calmness, a resolve, and—without a touch of makeup—a beauty that I had never seen before. She answered Judy, "Mom, I can't even begin to tell you how totally beautiful he really is." She went on to state that the colors she saw around Jesus were the most vibrant and vivid colors she had ever seen. Blues and reds and gold and every color of the spectrum took on a life of their own. And they were so intense that they were not colors like a book or on a wall, but living colors.

"While the light was intense, it did not blind me, which didn't make sense," she said. This was a brighter light than she had ever experienced in her 39 years, yet she was able to look right through it. She went on to say that Jesus told her he knew that she was in a lot of pain, and that she had suffered much, but that it would soon be all okay. Becky was not certain whether "Be okay" meant "be healed and stay here," or "Go to be with him." But she said it didn't really matter, because either way it was going to be okay.

Judy and I sat on either side of the bed and listened in amazement. We could not comprehend the utter sense of peace that had come over Becky. I cannot put into words or completely describe her state—it's as if she was radiating light.

As the disease process continued to take over her body, Becky maintained a peace and a calm that was unprecedented. It took our breath away.

As the end approached, Becky realized that her husband was going to be alone with her infant son. Her concern was for Ben and her husband. Judy and I were present when Becky turned to Judy and simply repeated the words that were spoken at Ben's birth barely a year prior: "Benjamin is yours now." As you can imagine, this was a very profound moment in which a mother who knows that there is nothing more that can be done turns her little son over to a loved one.

Within a few days of this event, on November the 7th, Becky left us, just two weeks prior to Ben's first birthday. All of the time that we had to experience and process this reality did not completely prepare us for the emotion we felt at her death. I don't believe, after my many years of dealing with loss, that I can say anyone is ever fully prepared.

It was comforting to us to know that Becky had, through her encounter with the Lord, some idea of what expect, and was able to share that with her loved ones. In spite of our grief and sorrow, we are comforted by Becky's own account of where she would be, and in her own words, that it was "going to be okay."

Stand Up Now, Walk, and Live

While serving in the US military, Pastor Jacobson chose to live off-base in Norfolk, VA. He was single at the time, and had a landlady who rented a room to him. Her name was Josephine Radcliffe. Pastor Jacobson met Josephine while attending a church where she was a member. After the service there was a church social, and he struck up a conversation with her. She indicated that she had a room for rent, and Pastor Jacobson decided that as a single man he would live off-base. This is the story as Pastor Jacobson told it to me:

"Josephine was an older lady who had never married and lived alone. A large woman, she had had numerous surgeries on her legs which restricted her primarily to a wheelchair for many years. The most I ever saw her walk was a few steps here and there. Her legs had atrophied to a point where they were not substantial enough to support a woman of her stature. She had wrapped them in ace bandages, and when her legs were unwrapped, they were extremely thin because of a number of surgeries. Doctors had indicated that her legs would never function properly due to tissue removal.

"Every evening, she would cook dinner for both of us. Being restricted in mobility, she would ask me to place food to be prepared on the counter to make it easier for her. She braced herself against a fixed object in the kitchen so she could stand erect while cooking. I marveled at her strong will and refusal to give in to her condition/situation.

"I drove Josephine to church on occasion, and one Sunday we heard that Katherine Kuhlman was coming to town. Ms. Kuhlman was known in Christian circles for her healing ministry.

"Ms. Kuhlman was born with a speech impediment. As a child, she was given therapy to help her enunciate and speak slowly so she would be intelligible to the standard listener. This slow approach to speech became her "calling card." She had a TV show in the 60s and 70s.

"She would come out on stage with dramatic long, flowing gowns analogous to Loretta Young. Josephine and I decided to try to see her at the Center Theatre in Norfolk. We went to the theatre and were able to secure tickets for the event. As was common for Ms. Kuhlman's appearances, people with disabilities were seated in a separate section of the venue to accommodate their ambulatory needs. Such was the case with Josephine.

"The evening started with praise and worship, followed by a music presentation by a Christian group or artist. Shortly thereafter, Ms. Kuhlman shared scripture on how to have faith and act upon it. One point that she stressed was that whatever miracles had and possibly would be performed were by the grace of God and by other faith in him, and not by her presence specifically. She focused on faith and the Holy Spirit.

"I sat with Josephine as we watched Ms. Kuhlman call people from the audience up to the stage. There was no specific format for her summoning. At times she would say, 'The Holy Spirit tells me that there are folks here with circulatory disorders. Please come forward.' Her staff would obtain the names of those who approached, and help them onto the stage, and Ms. Kuhlman would pray over them. Generally speaking, she would lay her hand on their head. Most of the time, those she was praying for would momentarily collapse in the arms of the staff.

"Josephine and I watched in amazement. Then something remarkable happened. Ms. Kuhlman stopped and turned in our direction. She proceeded to say, 'There is a woman in a wheelchair, you're unable to walk.' As I looked around, I saw many in women in wheelchairs. Then Ms. Kuhlman shouted, 'You are in row 52, seat 10.' For a split second, everyone started to check their seating position to see who it was. Amazingly, it was Josephine. Josephine looked at me and I looked at her. At that moment, Ms. Kuhlman instructed Josephine to get out of her chair and join her on the stage.

"It must be understood in the six months that I knew and lived with Josephine, I NEVER saw her take more than a few steps due to her condition. Again, Josephine was a large woman with tiny legs.

"Josephine sat there in a daze for a moment as Ms. Kuhlman continued to encourage her to stand up and walk to her. Without anything further being said or done, without any assistance whatsoever, Josephine stood up from her chair and proceeded very slowly towards the stage. At first she was very unsteady. It reminded me of a foal that is just birthed from its mother, wobbling and swaying. As she moved down the aisle, she became steadier, and increased her pace. I was completely astonished. As Josephine approached the stage, she was faced with the obstacle of the stairs she had to ascend to the stage surface. With the support of a staff member's arms, she walked up those stairs under her own power toward Ms. Kuhlman, something that she had not done in years.

"Josephine was simple in her approach, and said to Ms. Kuhlman, 'I thought you needed to pray for me and touch me.' Ms. Kuhlman chuckled and stated, 'I didn't have to pray and touch you—the Holy Spirit already did.' Further, she said, 'When you were called forward, you had to respond to your faith in God. You could have chosen to remain seated, or you could have done as you did and believed that you could do things that even the doctors said could not be done...Don't ever stop believing that God is able!'

"We left that night with Josephine walking, and she has walked ever since. I cherish a picture of her at my wedding some two years later: standing on her own and still walking. And Josephine walked until her death years later.

"Looking back on these experiences, I can see in one the trials and testing of a potential tragedy, and yet the tremendous joy of knowing that by never giving up my daughter was spared, how a young man's life was restored, and with Becky that a life after this one is tangible and available to anyone who puts their faith in Christ. It still amazes me that my landlady could walk for the first time in years because she stood on her faith.

My Week in Baltimore

I met Chelsea Leander while moving my daughter into her dorm at a popular southern university. I saw a young lady with a clipboard (a Resident Assistant), and asked her questions regarding the move-in rules. I had indicated that I traveled a long distance with my daughter's belongings in tow. I encountered extremely severe weather the first day, and only by the grace of God was I standing in front of her. Chelsea mentioned that she was a Christian, and that she was active in her youth group at the University. Here are her two stories. The first:

"I grew up in Charlotte, North Carolina. I volunteered to take a week-long mission trip for our junior high school to Baltimore, Maryland, which I got to help lead as a volunteer. Our bus was full, with a total of about 50 students and four adult leaders.

"One morning I took five of the students with me to hand out flyers announcing the Bible school as an outreach to local neighborhoods. One lady was watering her flowers as I walked toward her home. We greeted each other, and I stated my purpose. She responded that her children were grown, but that she did have grandchildren who she would send. I handed her the information, said a simple 'Thank you,' and began to walk to the next house, when the lady shouted to stop me before I got too far.

"She said, 'My name is Mrs. Blue. Would you please pray for me as you go? I have a doctor's appointment in about an hour to investigate some lumps they found that look cancerous.'

"I'm pretty sure that Mrs. Blue expected me to pray quietly alone somewhere, but instead I went and grabbed my team of five students, and returned to her house to pray right then and there. Mrs. Blue, her grandchildren, and our "team" of students held hands and prayed. When I opened my eyes, I saw that Mrs. Blue had tears streaming down her face.

Later that night, she came walking up to the church to pick up her grandchildren who had attended the Bible school. She came right up to me and said, 'You'll never believe what just happened:

not only do I not have cancer, but the doctor said that he couldn't find a single lump...they are gone!"

Mercy Ship

Chelsey's second story:

"At 18 years old, fresh out of high school, I was living in Africa on something called the Mercy Ship. The Mercy Ship's mission is to give hope and healing to the world's forgotten poor through the 2000-year-old example of Christ. They basically take poor people from around the world who have incredible medical problems and give them life-changing surgery for free while sharing the gospel with them so that they can take back hope to their village.

"One weekend, 12 crewmembers took a short 'shore leave' vacation while visiting the nation of Ghana. As we were driving down a mountain road in our 16-passenger van, another similar van sped by ours. We were very concerned for our own safety, because the only thing that prevented us from tumbling over the edge of the mountain to our deaths was a one-foot-tall guardrail. One lady from our group asked a crewmember named Paul to lead us in prayer. In my selfish mind, I was assuming that he was going to pray for our own safety. However, I was quickly surprised when I began to hear him praying for the safety of those in the van that had gone speeding by us.

"Within a minute we rounded a corner, and we were shocked to see the speedy van stopped on the side of the road with women sprawled out around it. As we drove by, it became obvious that the passengers, mostly women, were on their knees kissing the ground! We shouted out of our windows, asking: 'What happened?' and they responded, 'Our brakes failed! We had no way of stopping!' Driving by slowly, I stuck my head out the window and yelled, 'We prayed for you!'

"We were amazed as we passed this surreal scene. The van stopped...without brakes...on a steep mountain road. There was no reason for the van to have stopped on its own. As I witnessed this miracle, I began to realize that the power of prayer is real."

Massachusetts Miracle

Vernon and Sherrie Dawson operate the Wilderness Mission, a healing center located in the Berkshire mountain range, in the town of Savoy, Massachusetts. I was a guest of theirs when I was very ill, seeking help in rebuilding my mind and body. Vernon shared this amazing story with me.

Vernon and Sherrie Dawson travel quite a bit in their van. Vernon told me this story about what had happened five years before on a Saturday afternoon as they were going to Boston to put on a health presentation:

"We were traveling on a two-lane country road, with a river on the right-hand side and below us. We rounded a bend, and saw a large oil tanker tractor with trailer in the opposite lane coming in our direction. In an instant, the tanker-trailer started swinging out into our lane of travel.

"At that moment, I realized there was nowhere to go. So, in a split second I weighed the options. It seemed the only way out was to veer towards the river as if to go in. I cut the wheel and screamed: 'Lord help us!'

"Moments later, we opened our eyes, all shaken up, and I found us and our van stopped in the opposite lane of travel. There wasn't a scratch on us or on the van. This was impossible, as the tanker had been covering the entire road. We would have been surely crushed or killed without intervention. This was clearly a miracle."

My Angels Are With Me

I met David Simpson at the Wilderness Mission healing center in Savoy, Massachusetts. David had brought his 15-year-old son to the 10-day program to take a more natural approach to his juvenile diabetes. David had been born in Guyana, and had immigrated to Canada with his wife and children. He is a legal prosecutor. In the course of our stay, David prayed fervently with me. David has tremendous faith and a heart of gold. Here's his story:

"My name is Dave Simpson. I live in Canada. I had to complete my training as a machinist in order to become qualified. In order to complete the training, you are required to take a practical examination which consists of an instructor giving you dimensions to fabricate a precision device in just two hours. Each finished product had to be precise, and was examined by professionals using specific instruments to measure tolerances to the thousandths of an inch. I was very busy at the time, and was not able to study to the extent required.

"On the day of the test I found a quiet place, knelt down and asked the Lord to 'guide my hands' to allow me to program the sophisticated milling machine to achieve my goal and assure the instructors' satisfaction.

"I walked in and received my instructions. I completed my task, and passed. What is more amazing is that the faculty of the testing facility indicated that it had been done in record time: just 45 minutes. I know that it was the Lord who gave me the knowledge and was guiding my hands that day. There is no other plausible explanation."

My Mother's Unwavering Faith

I met John Kohler in a professional setting. He called on me in my capacity as a safety engineer. I knew something was different about him, and he was very open in regard to telling me two personal stories as follows:

"When I was in high school, my mother announced that she had been diagnosed with breast cancer. As you can imagine, this was a very scary time for her and for the rest of the family. The thought of losing your mother at any age is difficult, to say the least.

"My mother was an excellent example of a devout Christian woman. She prayed every day, and I know that those prayers included the Rosary, amongst other intentions. As an adult, I reflect on her kind and loving behavior, and feel completely blessed to call her "Mom." As my mother's physicians struggled with her life-threatening disease, they ordered a mastectomy. The doctors told her that a reoccurrence was a high probability, and that complications would be likely. She was treated both with chemotherapy and radiation to stop the progression. But Mom never wavered on her faith, and continued to pray fervently.

"One day I came home from school, and my mother greeted me at the door. I could see that she was elated. Her face was bright, and she was almost at the point of shaking. Without giving me a chance to ask her what was happening, she took me by the hand and said, "John, a miracle has happened!", then she led me over to the coat closet in our foyer where she always kept her purse.

"She took her purse out and removed a metallic set of Rosary beads she'd had for many years, and said, 'John, yesterday these beads were silver, and overnight all of them, except one, turned to a bronze color. And the one bead that didn't change was not tarnished at all. Nothing came into contact with the beads; nothing different was in my purse or this closet. I know this is a miracle." Right then my mother knew that it was a sign that her prayers had been heard.'

"My mother made a full recovery from her cancer, and beat the odds. God worked a miracle in her life. I am grateful to have my mother today. She inspired me in many ways.

"More recently, I have found many internet references of similar occurrences, referencing the appearance of the Virgin Mary in Medjugorje, Yugoslavia."

Faith is the Key: Austrian Drive

John Kohler's second story:

"My family moved to Vienna, Austria from Yardley, Pennsylvania when my father was working for RCA, which had been acquired by General Electric years before. My father was a consultant to the Austrian government, which at the time was building television stations in the capital city. I am the youngest of five children, and attended Austrian kindergarten and an American International School for five years before we returned to the United States.

"During our stay, our family took full advantage of living in central Europe, and traveled often to experience the history and splendor of the region. During one of our 'mini-vacations' we were driving at a high elevation in the Austrian Alps. My brothers and sisters were crammed in the back of a compact station wagon—cars are much smaller in general in Europe. The weather was bright and sunny at the start of our trip, and we were excited to see more sights.

"As we ascended into the mountains, the sky became grey and the weather started to become progressively worse. It started to rain heavily; the rain changed shortly to freezing rain (sleet), and then to a heavy snow. It was extremely slippery, and my father had difficulty controlling the car. We saw several crashes as we negotiated the hazardous switchbacks (most without guardrails). We became quite frightened, knowing that the car could easily slip off the side of the mountain, killing us instantly.

"My parents are devout Christians who practice the Roman Catholic tradition. While we were in the car on those zigzag roads, my mother turned to us and said, 'Children, let's recite the Rosary,' and we all started to pray: 'Hail Mary, Full of Grace, the Lord is with Thee, Blessed are thou amongst women and Blessed is the fruit of thy womb, Jesus. Holy Mary, mother of God, Pray for us sinners, now and at the hour of our Death.'

Just as soon as we recited the first verse, the car immediately came under control, even though the weather was still treacherous and slippery. We repeated this prayer over and over, and made safe passage to our destination.

"I know beyond a shadow of a doubt that our prayers were answered at that moment. I get goose bumps just thinking about how miraculous that time was, and it has never left my mind."

Asleep at the Wheel

Dr. Lee Cowden has been my personal physician during my healing journey. He took the time to tell me these two stories to bolster my faith.

Years ago, I was splitting my time between Texas and St. Louis, Missouri. I was working in a St. Louis hospital, and often made the 10-hour drive back and forth. As you can imagine, it was tiring to make the trip.

One night, I was not far from St. Louis, and I was very sleepy. It was late at night, and I was dozing off. I opened the car window and turned up the volume on the radio to try to stay awake. I did not want to pull over, because I had to be at the hospital shortly. I must have fallen asleep. In one moment, I felt a crack on the top of my head. I immediately woke up and found that I was headed right toward an embankment that preceded a bridge and the river below. Shaken up, I swerved back onto the road, then stopped and got out of the car. The car was undamaged, and had not struck anything. But the next morning, I awoke with a huge lump dead smack on the top of my head. No one else had been in the car, and I did not strike anything.

I firmly believe God or His angels woke me up that night to complete my work here. There is no other explanation.

The Tree

Dr. Cowden had a patient who related another automobile story. This narrative was paraphrased by Dr. Cowden.

My wife and I had taken a cross-country vacation in our pickup truck. We enjoyed several weeks on the road. On the last night of the trip, we were driving the last 20 miles to our home on a dark stretch of road late at night. Apparently I had fallen asleep at the wheel, and suddenly we veered off the road into the median. I awoke, and quickly struggled to recover the truck to make it back onto the highway.

My wife and I were both very shaken up, but we drove to our home and went to bed. The next day we decided to go back to that spot where we'd had our scary incident. We could see the tire tracks from where we went off the road, and went back up onto the highway. To our utter amazement, a large tree was in the dead center of the two tire tracks. We stood there speechless for what seemed like an eternity. We knew instantly that God had moved that tree for us.

Stop Now!

I was invited to run a 5K race one May sponsored by the Rhode Island State Police. Colonel Steven G. O'Donnell is a personal friend of mine, so I decided to do it. I struggled to run in spite of my weakened state, and near the finish I heard: "Don't let a fat guy beat you!" which was said by a younger guy named Brent. I thanked him for his encouragement, and asked him what he did for a living. He said he was a personal trainer at a specific gym. I was so taken with his kindness that I looked up the gym on the internet. When I opened the website, I was amazed at the quality and detail of the web page. At the bottom was the word "Mouseworks." I called and spoke with the owner, Jill Stevenson, about designing my website:

AngelsWalkingwithUs.net

In the process, she told me this amazing story. I firmly believe God leads us to people for a reason. Jill still manages my websites today. Here's Jill's story:

"I was about twenty-one, single, and heading home after another very busy day as a dental assistant for a group of oral surgeons. Driving my little yellow Austin-Healey Sprite, I was enjoying the ride and looking forward to seeing my boyfriend (now my husband) that late spring evening.

"As I made my way down one of the side roads that led to my parents' home, I remember looking at the corner where I was to take my right turn, perhaps 30 feet away. I was suddenly overcome by a "command" inside my head to 'STOP NOW!' I immediately slammed my foot on the brake...and less than two seconds later, a teenage boy flew around the corner on his bike and cut across the road in front of me. I was stunned. I would have hit him and surely hurt or killed him.

"I remember staying right there in my car for a few moments, trying to figure out why I stopped when I did, and thinking about the terrible future for both of us had I hit him. Perhaps someone had been watching over the boy, preventing him from being harmed so he could live his life and do the all things he was destined to do. Perhaps someone had been watching over me, too, so I didn't have to live my life with the knowledge and guilt that I'd harmed or killed someone. I'll never know. Yet all these years later, as I travel that same road and approach that same turn, I always say a silent 'Thank You!' to whoever was watching over us that day long ago."

Part IV

Divine Encounters

They say that sometimes God works in mysterious ways. The following stories illustrate His presence during miraculous, unanticipated visits. Here are truly amazing stories from people who have received His support and love when they least expected that gift.

A Priestly Visit

I was attending a professional conference in New Orleans in April of 2010. The conference was at one of the finer hotels in the area. As it happened, I was scheduled for a pre-conference workshop on Sunday afternoon. Hence, I arrived in New Orleans Saturday evening, and awoke early Sunday morning. I waffled about eating something, because I have been on a strict diet for years, and did not want to break it, but I knew I should eat before expending the energy the workshop would require. Being tired from the travel, I chose to eat in the hotel restaurant.

It was early, and the restaurant was very empty. A well-dressed, mature black woman appeared and greeted me. She told me her name was Jillian, and she was wearing a gold vest with a black bow tie. After exchanging pleasantries, she asked what I would like to eat. I started into my rendition of "I can't eat this and I can't have that." She looked at me and asked why. I proceeded to tell her about what I had been through medically and emotionally, ending by stating that I would never give up and had strong faith.

Jillian took my order and gave it to the chef, and then re-emerged to tell me about two events in her life that had given her unwavering faith and hope. The first story was about her:

Jillian told me that one day she became very ill. She could not balance herself and walk. She became nauseous, and her neighbor heard her calling for help. Jillian had little money, and truly could not afford any medical care, so she insisted to her neighbor that she be left alone. The neighbor would have none of it, and called for the rescue services.

When the medical technicians arrived, they indicated that she needed to be transported to the hospital immediately. Jillian persisted in stating that she had no money. The ambulance driver repeatedly told her that it was "go or die."

Jillian did not have money, but she had so much pride that to her, dying was a better option than not paying for that ambulance ride! To her surprise, the driver came over to her and said, "This one is on us, ma'am. Please, let's go now." Jillian yielded, and was admitted immediately to the hospital.

Doctors performed a series of routine tests, and an MRI of the brain. As it turned out, Jillian had a serious sinus infection that had penetrated her brain. It was a complicated and life-threatening infection, and a team of specialists needed to confer as to how to proceed. Since it was late in the day, nothing was going to happen that evening. The resident doctor notified Jillian that since she had no health insurance and the complications of surgery could produce weeks to months of recovery, it might not be an option for her. That night, she was put on high doses of antibiotics and anti-inflammatory drugs to contain the problem until doctors could truly assess the course of action on the following day.

Early in the evening, Jillian was visited by many doctors and nurses. Around 8 p.m., things started to quiet down. Her curtain was pulled around her bed. Jillian started to pray to the Lord. She asked for help and for healing. In a semi-lucid state, she noticed a pair of shiny black shoes below the curtain. She assumed it was another doctor making his final rounds for the evening. After watching the shoes for a minute, she quietly called for the person to enter. To her surprise, standing in front of her was a priest. He was Hispanic, and could not speak much English. He motioned to her to get out of the bed and stand with him. Slowly Jillian moved the IV lines and electrical leads to allow herself to stand on one side. The priest stood with her face-to-face, holding her hands for what seemed like about 15 minutes in deep prayer. He spoke softly, in Spanish, praying prayers and blessing her. Jillian grew weak, and he helped her back into the bed and left the area.

A few minutes later, her nurse came in to check on her vital signs. Jillian thanked her for sending in a priest for prayers.

The nurse looked puzzled and said, "I did not call for any priest."

"Please check with the floor nurses. I want to thank whoever called him in here," Jillian exclaimed. Her nurse returned, only to tell her it was a mystery because no one on the floor had called anyone, let alone a priest, to come to the unit. Jillian lay there, baffled but grateful, and soon fell asleep. The next morning, she was visited bright and early by a neurosurgeon.

"I have reviewed your MRI results," the surgeon told her. "You have a serious infection of the sinus and brain. I am ordering one more image of various areas of the brain and spine before we determine what course of action is feasible." Once more Jillian lay in the large MRI tube, listening to the hammering and buzzing noises made by the medical equipment.

Approximately two hours later, Jillian was resting in her bed, awaiting the results. The doctors came in cautiously, then with a direct and firm voice, told her that the infection had inexplicably "resolved." The doctors attributed it to a "rapid response" to the intravenous medications. However, nurses confirmed to Jillian that it was unheard of for a potential surgery case to "clear up" overnight. Within two days, the doctors released her without a scalpel ever touching her body.

In the following weeks Jillian called every church in the Greater New Orleans area to try to find the priest that had come to her bedside that evening. To her surprise, she was able to locate him in a Roman Catholic Church in a nearby community.

When she asked the priest through an interpreter, "Who told you to come see me?" he replied softly, "I have no idea why I came there to see you. I had a dream to go there, and asked God to direct me." She hugged him, and he blessed her. And that is her personal story.

Needless to say, while sitting in a near-empty dining room, I was mesmerized listening to this beautiful, mature woman. Jillian had great faith, and knew that I needed to hear one more account of God's great power.

I'll Be Just Fine!

As I sat there, Jillian took the time to tell me an additional inspirational story.

Jillian had a friend who worked in a drugstore chain not far from the hotel where I stayed. One day while at the drugstore, her friend received a call advising that her husband of 30 years had been taken by ambulance to the hospital, and that she needed to get to the hospital immediately.

Upon arriving, the woman saw her husband in a trauma room with a team of doctors and nurses wrapping up what looked like it had been a frantic time. In fact, they were. Apparently her husband had experienced a massive coronary, and the medical team had done all they could do to save him. He had not responded to defibrillation or injections to restart his heart.

She rushed to his side and held his hand as he lay lifeless in the trauma room. The doctors had slipped away, and the nurses left her to "say goodbye" to the love of her life.

According to Jillian, the woman told her husband, "I love you more than anything, sweetheart. You have been a good husband to me, and I will miss you forever. I'm so sorry I was not there when this happened. I love you!"

Then it happened. Her husband, now deceased for more than 20 minutes, sat straight up in the bed as if there was a rod in his spine. He looked directly at her and said in a strong voice, "Do not worry. Where I am going the water is so very clean and the fruit tastes so good." He then fell back on the bed, and was gone from this world forever.

Jillian's friend is happy today, knowing that her husband is safe in the arms of God in heaven, and that she will be reunited with him when her time comes.

My First Angel Flight

I was sitting in the in Phoenix airport, waiting patiently to board my flight back home after seeing Dr. Lee Cowden. It was a sad time for me, because my health was continuing to spiral downward. I felt like a complete and utter failure to my family during this time in my life because I couldn't be the husband and father I thought I should have been. I was weak and tired, and it sickened me to ask for a medical pre-board card at the gate. You see, I had to be near a bathroom, since I had to drink a gallon of water every day to help remove toxins from my body.

As I sat, I noticed an elderly lady being attended to by her daughter. They were laughing and carrying on loud enough for most of the gate area to hear. It struck me just how much these two really loved each other—the bond was palpable as they held hands and stared happily into each other's eyes.

The boarding announcement came sooner than expected, and mother and daughter embraced, kissing each other repeatedly. I deferred to my elder, and allowed her to board first as she waved goodbye to her daughter. I followed her to the first row, starboard side of the aircraft. She took the window seat, and I took the aisle so as to be near the lavatory. All of the other passengers embarked, and we took off.

I'm not certain what came over me shortly into the flight, but I became very emotional, to the point of sobbing. The elderly lady sitting next to me took one look at me and blurted out in a strong voice, "What's the matter?" I started to mumble that I had this and that, and within what seemed like a nanosecond she responded to me by saying, "Let me tell you a story." I quieted down and listened attentively.

She said, "My father and mother came here from Italy. We had a fruit store in the first-floor storefront of a six-tenement apartment building in Providence, Rhode Island. I was nine years old when my mother announced that we were going to have another sibling to play with. Later that year, it was time for the baby to be born. Eighty years ago, the doctor would come to the house to perform deliveries. "We all sat in the kitchen while the doctor was with my mother and father. We heard a lot of commotion for a good bit of time, and then my father appeared with tears in his eyes, holding my baby sister in his arms. He told us that Mom had died while giving birth. Next the doctor came out and asked that we wait a few minutes before we went in to see her so he could clean up the bedroom area. Naturally we were terribly sad to lose our mother. We entered the bedroom soon thereafter.

"As we stood quietly before her, my mother sat up from the bed with a sheet wrapped around her, and said the following words, to the astonishment of the doctor, my father and all of us: 'I have seen the Lord—he was writing in his book. The Lord said, 'You have seven children now. Go back, it's not your time.' My mother soon recovered completely, and lived another 40 years! She went to church every day for the rest of her life."

The elderly lady said, "There is nothing to be afraid of…Don't be afraid."

I sat there, stunned, as the lady went off to sleep for nearly the entire rest of the flight.

While she slept, a tall, good-looking male flight attendant was facing me as he was seated in his jump seat. I stared at him, and asked point-blank, "Have you been a flight attendant for a long time?" I still don't know to this day why I asked that question.

He looked at me and said, "No, just a year. You see, my 21-year-old son had passed away, and when he did I decided to do something that might make a difference. I like to help people now. I don't care how fancy the car I drive is, or how luxurious my clothes are. I just want to make a difference in this world. Everyone in that room when my son passed away has done the same. I can't explain it, but something came over all of us the moment he passed on. His mother and I are no longer together, but we have both made life changes to help others."

Now I sat there with my mouth wide open. Two complete strangers whom I would normally never have engaged in conversation told me these incredible stories of hope. As sad as I was, I know in my heart that God had sent two angels (later confirmed by Maureen Hancock) to give me direct messages to have faith and to never give up.

My Second Angel Flight

I again went to Phoenix to visit with Dr. Cowden. Although my health was still poor, I trusted that he could and would help me. On the flight home, an older lady took the window seat in the forward section of the aircraft, and I again took the aisle to have access to the bathroom.

I noticed the woman was reading a book—I believe it was about Mother Theresa. I struck up a conversation with her. She introduced herself as Marie Lessard. We started to speak of troubles and care of this world. Next thing I knew, Ms. Lessard told me that she had a sewing machine that embroidered cloth angels.

She said, "I think you need one...give me your address and I will send it to you." A few weeks later, as promised, a large envelope made its way to my mailbox. Inside there was a prayer card and a blue embroidered angel. I firmly believe that God put Ms. Lessard in front of me at that time. I felt hopeless and sad. But her words, her card, and the angel gave me the hope to continue my fight.

Mom Is with Me

I met Ron Zagarri in the most unbelievable manner. At the time, I was consulting with the state highway authorities about protecting workers in roadways. I had developed a few diagrams with the state traffic engineer that would be printed into books for drivers to keep in the cab of a truck.

About a week later, I received a telephone call at my office. The man on the other end of the phone said, "I print small booklets for all types of purposes. Can I be of any assistance?" I was taken off guard. "My name is Ron Zagarri," he said. We met for the purpose of printing highway safety books, and upon greeting each other, we recognized that there was much more to this new friendship. Here is Ron's story:

"I grew up in a close-knit Italian family from Boston. When I was 10 years old, my family took a trip to Montreal, Canada. My mother was blind, but insisted to my father that we stop at the famous Notre Dame Church. My father and I watched as my mother knelt down and prayed on each step until she reached the top. It took over an hour. I marveled at her faith and never forgot it.

"When my parents were elderly, my mother had been in and out of the hospital. On one Friday evening, my family made my mother's favorite dinner—spaghetti and calamari (squid)—because she'd had such a rough week health-wise. After she ate, she commented, "That was one of the best meals I ever had!'

"Mom's routine was to go upstairs and sit in her chair in her bedroom to relax. Mom was blind, so we took extra care to ensure that she was secure. As the evening progressed, my brother was about to leave to go home when he and my father heard a noise. They ran upstairs and found my mother sitting in her chair, unresponsive. The ambulance immediately brought her to the hospital.

"I received a call from my brother that Mom was being transported to the hospital and that I needed to be there. As I left my home, I sped towards the hospital and was stopped for speeding by the police. I pleaded with the officer to let me go, as my mother was very ill and I had to get to the hospital.

"When I arrived, my father and brother told me it was too late. My mother had passed away. It was very late, and since my father was elderly we agreed that my brother should take Dad home, and we would contact the funeral director in the morning.

"As my family departed, I asked the doctor if I could see my mother's body. I was led to a room where my mother lay motionless on a stainless steel table. I vividly recall that I held her hand in that quiet moment, and apologized for not seeing her before she left us. I thanked her for all she had done for me, and told her that I loved her. With a kiss, I bid her goodbye and went home.

"At the time, I lived on the edge of the Atlantic Ocean. My backyard was literally a rock cliff. I had a large sliding window that gave me a panoramic view of the sea from my bedroom.

"I sat on the edge of my bed and stared out into the moonlit water. I thought about my mother and the kindness and love she had poured out to me and all that knew her. At that moment, what I can only describe as a green ball of fire appeared outside the window.

"It hovered there for a moment, and then entered my bedroom. I sat there, pinching myself to see if I was dreaming. I was not.

"An overwhelming sense of peace came over me as the amazingly brilliant fireball was suspended in front of me. I knew right then and there that it was my mother saying 'goodbye.' As soon as it came, it went away from me, streaming over the open sea.

"My thoughts and my life have been forever changed. I am not afraid at all, and can't wait to see my mother again. Thank you, Mom!"

Mike the Barber

Mike was introduced to me by Ron Zagarri and I personally interviewed Mike. He was a spry 71-year-old barber of Italian descent. He has worked hard all his life, and is, in my opinion, a good humble man, upstanding citizen, and of sound mind. This is his story:

"My name is Mike Colarusso, and I am a hair stylist in the town of Swampscott, Massachusetts. I have been a stylist for 50 years, styling both men's and women's hair. I have worked 10 hours a day all my life to support my family.

"Many years ago, I met Mrs. Beatrice "Bebe" Silverman, who became a client, and later a close friend of my family. Early in my practice (35 years ago), Bebe asked me if she could be my receptionist for a few days a week. She in fact was for a period of three years.

"Twice a week, Bebe would come to the salon to have her hair done. A few months ago she spoke to me when no one else was in the salon and said, 'I have something I want to tell you. I have not told anyone else....They will think I'm crazy. My friend's son died unexpectedly at the age of 45. Out of respect for her, my husband and I went to the Roman Catholic Church to his funeral service. As I sat there in the pew, I saw a statue of a saint (I'm not sure which one) with its hands moving towards itself, in a motion of calling, as if it was saying, 'Come to Me.' I didn't say anything to anyone, because they would have thought I was crazy.'

"Bebe asked me what I thought it meant, and wanted to know if what she saw was real. I told her I believed that what she had seen was very real and that she shouldn't be scared, but to understand that it was something good which happened to her.

"Three weeks later, she fell in her kitchen, and died a day later after a brief coma. Her husband, Mr. Silverman, called to tell me that she had passed away.

"I believe that God was sending her a message that it was going to be okay and not to worry. Although Bebe didn't understand it at the time, I knew that it was a message to her.

135

"I am very ill now, and undergoing cancer treatments. Even with all the pain and suffering I am enduring, I am not afraid. Thank you, God, for having Bebe tell me that story. I know you are with me always."

Mike passed away a few weeks after telling me this story. I completely believe we were destined to meet and his story was to be included among the others in this book.

Kendall: I'm Pleased to Meet You

I met Jennifer Dionne when I was at one of the lowest points in my life. Jennifer is a private detective that lives and works in Rhode Island. This is what Jennifer told me:

"I had an uncle named Jimmy Neuhoff, who was very hard of hearing due to a childhood illness. We were close to one another, and I called him every day.

"A few years after I was married, I learned that I was pregnant. My husband and I were very excited, and when we found out we were having a baby girl, we started the process of selecting potential female names.

"I called Uncle Jimmy that day, and told him in a very loud voice that we had three prospective names picked out: Kendall, Sloan, and Lacey. There was a long pause before he responded in his booming voice, 'Oooh, Dolly, I don't think you want to name a baby Slow and Lazy. You should go with Kendall!'

"Uncle Jimmy passed away before my daughter was born. Here is what my daughter Kendall has to say about Uncle Jimmy."

Kendall's Story:

"When I was three years old, I was in sleeping in my bedroom. I woke up and saw a man I did not recognize. I was not frightened for some reason, because he seemed familiar, but I did not know why.

"I went back to sleep, and when I woke the next morning, I described what I had seen to my mom. 'He had kind, gentle eyes, and was well over six feet tall with a mustache,' I told her. She said it sounded like her uncle Jimmy who had passed away when she was pregnant with me.

"I went to my Nona's (term for grandmother) that day, and saw a picture of him on the refrigerator. I knew that this was the man I had seen. My uncle knew my name before I was born, and I believe he was looking forward to the birth. He used to ask my mom how his little dolly Kendall was when they spoke on the phone almost daily.

"I feel his presence sometimes; it's hard to put into words. Like others that have passed over, he leaves pennies, and I find them in places they should not be, or where they weren't a moment before.

"My mom remembered him singing the lyrics, 'Every time it rains, it rains pennies from heaven'"... and I'm convinced he's sending them to me."

My Father and His Blue Suit

Chip Thomas, a colleague of mine, offered two stories for this book. Chip and his sister organize a fund raiser each February to raise money for a national charity that provides education and research for heart health. Both of Chip's parents died of heart disease, nine months apart. Here's his first story:

"My father became quite sad after my mother passed away. He continued to try to assume his normal routine, which consisted of driving to his barber shop each and every day. At one point, he knew that he was failing, and called me over to him.

"He said, 'Chip, I want to be buried in my blue suit.'

"I answered, 'Of course, Dad, whatever you want.' Well, the day soon came when Dad passed away. My sister Patty and I went into his home at the request of the funeral director to obtain his burial clothing. Patty and I searched the bedroom closet without finding any sign of the blue suit. All that was present was a black suit.

"I vividly recall looking up to the ceiling and saying, 'Dad we can't find any blue suit. I guess you'll have to enjoy the black one.'

"A few weeks later, Patty and our spouses planned a return to Dad's place to start the process of dividing up personal effects. Patty and I were the only two people who had keys and access to the home. She made her way to the bedroom, and within a minute or so, my wife and I heard a scream. We rushed into the bedroom to find Patty standing in disbelief as she stared into the closet. There in the center of the closet was my father's blue suit. We stared at one another in shock.

"When we took it down and checked it, I found a photograph of my father and mother embracing in the inner pocket. I cannot explain any of this, but I know that God can create miracles."

A Night Out that I Will Never Forget

Here's a second story by Chip Thomas:

"My wife, Fran, and I needed an 'emotional break' one weekend, and we decided to head to a local casino. Fran loves the slot machines, and I just like to smoke a cigar and have a glass of brandy. We generally split up, and I find a corner where I enjoy my vices and people-watch. We circle back from time to time, where she updates me on her progress.

"One particular evening, I was feeling very melancholy about the loss of my mother and my father within less than a year of each other. As I sat in a comfortable chair in the casino, I noticed a man sitting next to me, who was probably in his late 50s or early 60s. He was dressed like a Vietnam War veteran and had long hair.

"This stranger looked at me and said, 'Things are not so good, are they?'

"Somewhat surprised, I replied, 'No, they are not. I'm a little sad.' Somehow we struck up a conversation, and I talked about my parents passing away within a short time of one another.

"This man's response was, 'I died myself once—it was amazing and beautiful.' He had mentioned that he played in various blues bands with artists who had long since passed away. 'I did not want to come back,' he continued, 'but I was compelled to come back here.'

"I sat there in total shock. He went on, 'It's going to be all right.' I looked down for a brief moment (three seconds or so), and when I turned my head to address the stranger, he had vanished. I scanned the area, but he was nowhere in sight. I could not believe what had just happened, but know now that he was sent to me to let me know that my parents are in a better place."

The Early Appointment

I met Tim Lang in the course of doing business. He was a soft-spoken, tall, lanky man with curly hair. His company supplied services to our firm. We met annually to review our contract and discuss general issues. He knew of the illness that plagued my body. We were at lunch one day in the cafeteria when I told him I was writing a book that included stories many to me about faith and belief.

He stared at me and said, "Here are two more stories."

"My name is Tim Lang, and I've been married to my wife Nancy for 20 years. Nancy had had the same OB-GYN since before marriage. She always went for an appointment the first week of April, which coincided with her birthday. She received a written notice for the appointment each year, and in 1998, she received the card in late January for an appointment in early February, two months early. Initially, she was upset, and was concerned that medical insurance might not cover an early visit. Notwithstanding, she decided to keep the unusually early appointment. She based this decision on what a nightmare she thought it would be to attempt rescheduling a visit.

"At her exam, the doctor detected a small growth in her left breast, and performed a biopsy. The doctor had strong suspicions that the growth was cancerous, but cautioned Nancy to wait for the test results. The doctor called within a short time to confirm his suspicion, and in fact this was an aggressive form of melanoma cancer.

"After surgery, I met with the doctor who told me that within the ten days from the office visit to the day of surgery, the tumor had grown from the size of a pea to the size of a walnut. The doctor indicated that Nancy was fortunate to have been diagnosed early, thereby averting the unthinkable.

"The doctor never knew that her appointment notice was early by two months. Of course, had Nancy not kept the early appointment, the circumstances would have been drastically different. Nancy followed the surgery with a year of chemotherapy and radiation treatments, and has to date successfully been cancer-free after 12 years. I know that it was a direct intervention and not an error that the card arrived early."

David Can See!

Tim Lang also had another amazing story. His nephew, David, was born in April of 1975. This is Tim's story:

"David was born with webbed fingers on one of his hands, and also born with an undeveloped optic nerve. His parents became suspicious when he was several weeks old that he might be blind, because he did not follow or react to motions that they made. His parents took him to a major US medical center specializing in vision disorders for an evaluation. Doctors told his parents that David's optic nerve was not developed, and that David would never have sight. In addition, his parents were instructed to register him as blind so that assistance would be available for training and development for someone with this malady.

"Tom's aunt Alice was a nun in the order of The Sisters of the Presentation of Mary. Sister Alice learned of David's condition, and indicated that she would pray for him daily. The Sisters of the Presentation of Mary had been founded by Mother Rivier. Here is the information about the founder from their website:

"Marie Rivier, fondly known as Marinette, was born December 19, 1768 in Montpezat, France. At the end of April, 1770, Marinette, then sixteen months old, had a bad fall which left her handicapped. Her mother, a woman of great faith, carried Marinette to the statue of the Pieta each day. Soon the little girl, who watched her mother pray, was certain: 'The Blessed Virgin will cure me!'

Finally, on September 8, 1774, Marinette began to walk! These four years of "schooling" with the blessed virgin Mary transformed Marie Rivier's life forever.

"By the age of eighteen, Marie was devoting herself to evangelization and to the care of the poor. She even opened a school, despite the reluctance of the pastor, who was soon reassured. Marie's zeal to make Jesus known extended beyond the classroom to the adults in the community. When the French Revolution broke out and every religious action was suspicious, Marie Rivier secretly held Sunday assemblies. She was cautious, but remained an apostle with a heart of fire.

"In 1794, the village of Thueyts beckoned her, and she willingly responded. Soon four young women joined her. At a time when all the convents were being closed, Marie Rivier opened hers. On November 21, 1796, the feast of the Presentation of Mary in the Temple, Marie and her four companions consecrated themselves to God. The new community grew very quickly despite the poverty it experienced.

"For Marie Rivier and the young women who worked with her, the Christian education of youth was and will remain a priority. However, religious education extended to adults as well. The poor also held a special place in Marie's heart, and she opened her first orphanage in 1814. Even if the house was poor, welcoming the most destitute was sacred.

"When she died on February 3, 1838, this woman-apostle with a heart of fire had founded 141 houses, and had received more than 350 Sisters to continue her mission. Marie Rivier, 'a prophet for our time,' was beatified in Rome by Pope John Paul II on May 23, 1982."

"Sister Alice received a relic of Mother Rivier when she became a nun in the order. She then sent the relic to Tom's mother for the express purpose of blessing David with the same. On the morning the relic arrived, Tom's father, who was a quietly devoted man, took the relic and read the information that came with it, then held it to his eyes with a prayer that David's sight might be restored. He went on his way to work as a daytime truck driver.

"Later that day, David's father Ben woke David and took him from his crib after his midday nap. Ben was sitting in a chair holding David, relaxing with a drink, when David reached for the can in his hand. Ben immediately knew that this was highly unusual, and called his wife, Sue. Both parents brought David out into the sunlight where he started blinking and focusing on objects in the yard. Both parents became excited and immediately returned to the medical center to discuss this turn of events. The doctor initially cautioned them not to be overly confident, as they had believed David's condition was irreversible. Later testing then revealed that in fact David's sight had been somewhat restored. Doctors had no medical explanation.

"Sue called her mother to tell them the good news, and her mother then called her husband at the trucking office. Immediately upon answering the telephone, he asked, 'David can see, can't he?' which was a stunning statement. In addition, Ben called his mother, who was traveling on the West Coast at the time. She also answered the telephone the same way: 'David can see, can't he?' Her statement was based on a premonition she'd had while attending a church service earlier that day. We cannot explain the miracle."

Guardian Angel-Nana Camara

I met Rose Barboza several years ago. She is a seventy-some-thing, a "sparkplug" and an amazing Christian. Rose's story follows:

"Many years ago in the 1960s, my husband left, leaving me with five children. I worked from 11pm-7am as a nurse at a general hospital in Massachusetts to support my children. Shortly after my husband departed, I started feeling ill, and made an appointment with my doctor, Dr. Benjamin Levitt, who has since passed away.

"He examined me and said: 'Rosemary, you need to be admit-ted to the hospital tomorrow and have a surgical procedure. You have cancer of the uterus.'

"I said, 'Doctor Levitt, I have five children. I can't just leave them and go to the hospital!'

"He replied, 'If you don't, you will not be able to take care of them, and they won't have a mother.' Needless to say, I was shocked and feeling complete disbelief. I thought this was a bad dream. The doctor continued to make arrangements for me to be admitted.

"That day I went to my pastor, Reverend Emery of the con-gregational church. He was a special pastor, a tall, gangly man with a gentle manner. The Pastor had helped my son Jim, a Boy Scout, obtain his 'God and Country' award for scouting.

"I told the Pastor what Dr. Levitt had said to me. I asked the Pastor for help. I needed someone to watch my children while I underwent surgery in the hospital. The Pastor suggested I place my children in a home for a period of time.

"I immediately recoiled, and blurted out, *'I'd rather die first than leave my children with others!* They were rejected by their father, and I will not allow them to be rejected again, ever.' I went home and made dinner for the children, never revealing the horror, fear, and anxiety I was experiencing in my heart. I put them to bed by kissing them and tucking them in that night, and I listened to their prayers.

"As absurd as it may sound, for some reason I started to clean my home. I had it in my mind that if I was going to die, that whoever came to my home would find it clean. I had tears streaming down my face going about my task. Afterwards, I sat at the kitchen table, crying, with my face in my hands, and said, "God, please help me." At that time I didn't have a personal relationship with the Lord, but I did believe.

"I can't recall how long I sat there crying, but I heard a knock on the door. There in the doorway stood a woman who attended my church, named Isabel Camara. She said, 'God has given me the privilege of watching five beautiful children while you go to the hospital.' I cried and gave her a huge hug.

"I said to her, 'I don't know how long I'll be in the hospital, and I have no money to pay you. My income is just enough to survive, to feed my children.'

"She said, 'Don't worry. God takes care of everything, sweetheart.'

"It is a miracle that this happened, because I never knew Mrs. Camara any more than to say good morning to her in church. Mrs. Camara changed the flowers in church and cooked for the ill, and was truly a Godly woman.

"I showed her the children's rooms and the rest of my home. I had the children's lunches packed for school the next day, and the clothes out on the bed for the next morning.

"Mrs. Camara restated, 'Don't worry, sweetheart. Send the children off to school, and I will take care of everything. I will also visit you and keep you informed.'

"The next morning I sent the kids off to school. I gave them hugs and kisses, and never said a word about what was to come. I made that conscious decision because I knew in my heart that I would break down in front of them, and that would create fear for my kids.

"I locked the door to my empty home, and with my little suitcase in hand got into my jalopy of a car and drove off to the hospital. I was admitted and had the surgical procedure. Doctors monitored me closely, and I spent to a total of six weeks there. I lost 31 pounds in the process, leaving my total weight at a paltry 68 pounds!

"While I was in the hospital, Mrs. Camara came to see me after church on Easter Sunday. To my surprise, the children were in tow. The kids wore the dresses and capes I had made for them, complete with straw hats and white gloves. My youngest was my son Scott, who was only two at the time, and he wore knee socks with white shoes. All of them looked adorable. What a blessing that Mrs. Camara and her daughter Margie (who is my dearest friend to this day) came in my time of need, by the grace of God. All I did was ask.

"I recall the scripture: 'Ask not and ye shall have not.'

"My daughter Christal started to cry when it was time for the visit to end. And she said, 'Please, Mommy, don't die!' and I hugged and kissed her and told her Mommy would not die, Mommy would soon be home. I knew from that moment on that I was going to recover completely.

"Before I was discharged, I had met another patient named Irene Talbot. I was bedridden for many weeks, and this kind woman Irene made it a point to offer me a warm washcloth and talk with me. The day I was able to move about, I asked that I be transported to her room via wheelchair to surprise her.

"When I arrived in her room, she was shocked and elated to see me. Her daughter happened to be in the room.....her name was Judy Kirkwood, a beautiful young lady who was dressed impeccably. Judy indicated she was a district manager for Avon, and mentioned that there were possibilities for income in Avon sales. I told Judy that I was not a salesperson, but I thanked her for the offer.

"Upon convalescing, I gave some thought to Judy's offer, and decided to become a representative for Avon. After school and on Saturdays, I piled my five kids into a car, threatened them so they would behave, packed snacks, and went door to door selling Avon products. Mrs. Gifford was my district manager. We attended a sales meeting, and in the process I met Shirley Corliss. I had no idea that Shirley was a VIP in Avon; I assumed she was a representative like myself.

"I was very successful and kept to a schedule. Eventually, I received a telephone call from Bob Vinton of Avon, who was a Corporate Executive in New York. He mentioned that he had spoken with Shirley Corliss regarding a position for district manager in my area, and said he would like to interview me. He asked me to meet him in a Massachusetts hotel.

"I responded, 'If you think I'm that good, then you will meet me at a place I select.' He laughed heartily. We met at my home, and Mr. Vinton discussed his interest in sending me to an Avon development/ marketing school in New York City for a week. I found out that the pool of candidates numbered 32. During our conversation at the house, I mentioned to him that I had children who could not be left alone. He responded by offering to pay for a babysitter, and offered me a large sum of money at that time should I accept.

"I prayed about this with Mrs. Camara, and decided to go. I arrived in New York a complete country bumpkin, who wore little or no make-up, with these stylish 31 women. We learned and competed all week in various skills.

"Mr. Dick Chapin, who was the director of the program, called me into his office at the close of the week, and said, 'We have chosen you for this position!'

"I paused to let his words sink in, and then blurted out, 'I have to think about this, because, Mr. Chapin, I am a mother first, and this is a real career. I need to go home and pray about this.'

"Mr. Chapin was shocked. He said, 'Those women out there would sell their mothers to have this position, and you have to think about it!'

"I responded by saying, 'If I take this position, I will do my very best, but I am a mother first.' I departed New York City, and prayed about it all weekend. On Monday morning I called Mr. Chapin, and told him that I would take the job and do my very best.

"Over the next 27 years, I became a 'Circle of Excellence' Avon manager, with many successes. It was an accomplishment to achieve this level once. But by the grace of God, it happened for me seven times! I won trips, made inroads in Avon processes, and contributed much to this growing organization.

"God had a plan for me....And through it all, fear, loss, anxiety, loneliness, and thoughts of death plagued me. God put me in front of Irene Talbot and her daughter in the most unlikely place—a hospital room. That experience changed my life. I am still dearest friends with Judy today, and we are both retired Avon managers.

"The most important reflection of all I have and know is that my faith in God brought me to where I am today. And it started with that knock on the door from my guardian angel, Nana Camara, who God sent when I was in despair. I know that when it is my time, I will see Nana at the gates of heaven.

"All that I am and ever hope to be I owe it all to thee."

Peace: A Gift from God

When I was 17 years old, I met Jim Russo at the fire station where I spent seven years volunteering as a firefighter and emergency medical technician. Jim and I bonded through our experience of saving lives and witnessing devastating loss. The ride to and from the area hospital was often an hour or more round trip. So you really get to know someone in those many hours spent together.

When he found out that I was very ill, he made it a point to call me often, even though I had not seen him in years. When he discovered that I was writing a book to offer hope, he stepped up and shared two very personal stories. Jim has the highest level of integrity, and I respect him immensely. This is Jim Russo's story:

"My daughter Kimbley grew up like any other normal child: happy, healthy, and full of life. At the age of 18, my daughter was married, and later had three children.

"She became very ill one spring when she was 36. It was very uncharacteristic for Kim to complain. She sought medical attention at a local physician's office to try to determine what was happening to her. She became very frustrated because she went into and out of medical facilities for nearly a year with little success in diagnosing her mystery illness. What made matters worse was that she was reluctant to seek additional medical advice, because she had only basic medical insurance coverage.

"In the interim, Kim had gallbladder surgery and pancreatic surgery, a result of testing which showed abnormalities in those organs. The doctors were perplexed, because no one could diagnose her.

"Just before Christmas, Kim was so ill again that she had to be admitted to the hospital. Days turned into weeks, and weeks turned into a month. Of course, nobody wanted her in the hospital for an extended period of time, because she was not a high-paying patient. Just as soon as doctors believed she was stable enough to be released, they sent her home.

151

"Eight weeks later, Kim became violently ill again, and was again readmitted, and again received the normal battery of tests. Her stay was extended again another four weeks. At that point, Kim was in excruciating pain, and her vital organs had started to fail. Her body was very weak. Doctors appeared to be clueless.

"Once she was stable enough, the doctors ordered her to a nursing rehabilitation facility to help her assimilate back into her normal routine and function. Those plans were set on a Friday for a Monday hospital discharge. That Monday, on the day of her discharge, we received a call that Kim had slipped into a coma.

"My wife, Sandie, and I returned to the hospital to see our daughter on a life-support ventilator, unresponsive. The doctors had run out options, and started intimating the inevitable. We were told that Kimbley would not awake from her comatose state. After much discussion, it was agreed that our family would gather on that Friday to say our goodbyes. Kim had not improved or shown any change in condition during that week, just as the medical staff had predicted.

"The immediate family, which included our son-in-law, siblings, grandparents, aunts and uncles, and of course Sandie and myself, gathered in the room. After everyone left, we circled around her hospital bed. Her siblings, a brother-in-law, myself and Sandie were at her bedside, when, amazingly, Kim opened her eyes. She looked over at Sandie and I, and then over to her two sisters, and then looked back at Sandie. Sandie insists that it was a look that said: "Mom, I have had enough," and then she closed her eyes forever.

"Reflectively, I now know that she was saying goodbye, and that brief moment allowed us to know that she was 'okay,' and that it was time for her to go. I believe my daughter knew that both Sandie and I needed that assurance or our lives would have been bitter, dark, and empty forever. I thank God for that gift.

Dad! Who are You Speaking To?

Jim Russo also offered this story about his father's encounter with God:

"My father, Edward Russo, was a social worker for the State of Rhode Island for 30 years. He was married to my mother for over 50 years. My father suffered a heart attack in his 40s, and basically lived on 'borrowed time' for another three decades. At the age of 79, he was hospitalized with congestive heart failure. He went to the hospital on Thanksgiving Day, waiting until after the meal to tell us to call for an ambulance. Dad remained in the hospital until he passed away on December 10th.

"I was working the day before he passed away, so my wife Sandie spent eight and a half hours in his room keeping him company. Sandie loved my father. They had become quite close when Sandie was relegated to living with my dad and my mom for a period of 10 weeks as she convalesced from an injury. As Sandie prepared to depart for the evening, my Dad looked at her point blank, and stated that he 'refused to let go' until his brother Joseph arrived from Florida. Struck by that comment, she kissed him goodbye and left for the evening.

"The next morning, the family was hastily summoned to the hospital. The doctor had called, indicating that it was apparent that Dad was not long for this world. My mother, myself, my kids and in-laws were all alerted to head to Dad's bedside. By the time Sandie and I arrived, my father was semi-comatose. I cannot completely verbally describe the scene I saw when I entered. Dad's eyes were fixed straight up on the ceiling. He was speaking very softly, saying words that were unintelligible.

"Sandie asked him, 'Dad...Who are you talking to?'

"At that moment, Dad turned his head and looked straight at her, saying 'I'm talking to God.' My wife and I were shocked, because my father did not believe in any afterlife. He never uttered another word to anyone else.

"My wife and I left the room briefly to take a break. We descended to the lobby level, and within a minute my daughter

153

came down screaming that Grandpa had died. When we entered his room, I stared directly at his face, seeing what I can only describe as the most peaceful face I have ever seen on anyone in death. Remember, George and I had seen plenty of death in our years of emergency medical service. I had never seen that peace on anyone else before, and I haven't since.

"The more amazing part of this story is that back in those days, cell phones were not allowed in the hospital because it was unclear whether the signal would cause interference with medical devices. In addition, the earlier cellular phones were primitive in nature, and did not have the voice recording capabilities of today's smart phones. I had decided to leave my phone in the drawer of the nightstand, and it was completely powered off.

"After Dad passed away, we gathered our belongings (which included the phone), and got into the car for the ride home. I turned on my cell phone before I headed out of the parking lot, and noticed I had a voicemail message waiting. I retrieved my message, and to my shock and surprise, every word that was spoken in that room in our absence was repeated on that voicemail message, specifically the doctor pronouncing my father deceased.

"For starters, it was impossible for this device to record, secondly the message was not sent from another phone. There is no question in my mind that my father wanted to let us know what transpired when Sandie and I left that room. We both listened to the message twice, and then it inexplicably disappeared from my phone.

"My father's angels allowed us to listen, and to know that Dad left peacefully. I thank God that I had this message sent to me. I have always believed, and this helped me know that Dad is okay."

The Volcano

I met Julie several years ago when our kids played sports together. She and her family were new to the area, and I had baked a plate of cookies to welcome them.

One day on the soccer field, I noticed Julie was crying and asked her what was wrong. Julie indicated that she had just received a call that her father, who lived in another state, had passed away that morning. I held her and told her, "It will be all right." Several years later, she told me this story:

"I lived in a beautiful home. My master bedroom and bath were the size of a small back yard. On my dressing table was a warm paraffin wax bath. It is a typical device used by many women to help soften the hands. I had used the wax bath for years, and it always sat in the same location.

"It had been several years since my father had passed away, and I had been feeling upset and sad that my marriage of nearly two decades was coming to an end. One morning in the fall, when the house was quiet, I was arranging items in my bedroom drawers. I came across my father's prayer card issued from the funeral home. I stared at it and felt strange feelings. Just then, the wax bath started to erupt and gurgle like a volcano for what seemed like an entire minute. This never happened before or since.

"I know for certain that my father was sending me a message that he was OK. I will never forget that moment, ever. I completely believe that God sends us messages through our departed loved ones."

With Prayer, Anything Is Possible

Here is another accounting from Pastor Jacobson:

"While living in Virginia, our family started to attend Friends Church in Portsmouth. The Pastor of the Church, Frank Carter, introduced me to Lloyd Bolt, whom he had known for many years. Lloyd had attended Pastor Carter's church in Eden, NC. When Pastor Carter relocated to Virginia, Lloyd and his family sold everything and moved along with the Pastor to his new congregation.

"While in North Carolina, Lloyd had been a firefighter, and was a proficient investigator. Upon relocating to Virginia, he accepted a position with the Occupational Safety and Health Administration.

"Lloyd had always had an affinity for the Hispanic population. He would often assist Hispanic workers by sending funds to their families, and he helped them find adequate housing and medical care, etc. One day I received a call from Lloyd that a young 20-something Hispanic migrant worker had had a serious industrial accident. Apparently, the worker suffered major trauma, including a punctured lung and broken bones, and he was unconscious. Of course Lloyd was aware of the situation through his professional capacity with OSHA. The worker was transported to one of the hospitals in Norfolk, Virginia, where he was put on a ventilator. In the course of the diagnostic testing, it was determined that the worker had no brain activity. Due to the seriousness of his injuries, his family was summoned from Mexico.

"In the interim, Lloyd asked me to meet him at the hospital. We met in the lobby, where he briefed me on the seriousness of the worker's condition, and asked me to pray with him over the worker in the Intensive Care Unit. When we arrived at the ICU, I noticed that each patient was in a 'cubicle' rather than separated by the old-style curtains so commonly used years before. When we entered, I was struck by this very handsome young man lying in the bed with the appearance of merely being asleep. In my mind's eye, I had expected to see large bandages and obvious signs of trauma. That was not the case.

"Lloyd explained that the doctors had felt there was little hope for this young man, hence the reason for summoning the family with the intention of returning his body to his homeland for interment.

We prayed over this worker not once but twice in the course of several hours. Each prayer time in the hospital consisted of Lloyd on one side of the bed and myself on the other. We prayed fervently for as long as we could the first time before being told to move on, since this was the ICU and the patient needed attention. We continued to pray outside of the ICU, and it appeared that the patient's status was unchanged.

"Lloyd called again a day later to indicate that the family had arrived, and asked that I once again meet him at the hospital to pray over the worker. When I arrived, the family had not yet made it to the hospital, but were en-route. Lloyd and I again entered the cubicle to pray. Lloyd explained to me that the young man's EEG was flat-lined, and that the life support was continuing for the benefit of his family. The physicians intended to remove him from the same as soon as the family had personal time with him.

"We took our places on opposite sides of the bed, praying over this man. I can't remember exactly what I prayed, but was later informed by Lloyd that I had asked God to 'perform a Genesis work' in this young man. While we were still in the room, the charge nurse entered and indicated the family had arrived.

We stepped out, and Lloyd greeted the mother and wife of the patient. Lloyd spoke fluent Spanish, and was able to detail who he was and what had happened to their husband and son. At one point, the mother and wife mistook me for the doctor. Lloyd explained that I was a personal friend of his, and was here to pray over their son and husband.

"The charge nurse then asked Lloyd to interpret to the family that this was their opportunity to spend time with the patient before the life support systems were removed. There was still no brain activity and no hope for recovery.

"Lloyd and I removed ourselves, and waited a short distance away to give the family their privacy. Several minutes later we heard screaming and crying coming from the ICU cubicle. Lloyd and I looked at each other, assuming that the young man had died.

"As the commotion continued, we entered the cubicle along with the nurse, only to discover that the young man was sitting upright in the bed, and had pulled the endotracheal tube out of his mouth and throat himself to speak to his mother and wife in Spanish. The young man was doing all the talking, and Lloyd, the nurse, and I were in shock. Needless to say, we were speechless.

"After a split second, the nurse called for a doctor, stat. The routine of the ICU was changed for the rest of the day. Over the next few weeks, the young man's condition continued to improve. Today he has normal brain activity, but is paralyzed from the waist down. He is able now to hold his little baby in his arms and hug his wife and his mother. This man was dead! Never underestimate the power of prayer. Never. Miracles happen every day.

"Lloyd has since gone to be with the Lord. He never considered his occupation to be just a job, but rather he saw it as a means for him to reach out and enrich others' lives both physically and spiritually. In this particular case, he was able to accomplish both."

I Met God

I met Beverly on a flight back home from Dallas, Texas. She works as a flight attendant for a major U.S. airline. As she asked me for my drink order, I commented on the angel pin attached to her apron. She indicated there was a special story attached to her wearing that pin, and said she wanted to share it. Here is her story:

"I was born in England, and was raised there until the age of 15½. At that time, my parents decided to emigrate to the U.S. My mother was a nurse, and there were more opportunities back then for her and my family in the States than in the UK. So I, my two sisters, my brother and my parents left England and arrived in Salt Lake City, Utah, where my mother had arranged employment.

"It was an adjustment for me, as I attended a public high school in Utah which was coed. In England, my school had been girls only, with uniforms required and strict rules. I had to make new friends, and felt awkward and unsure of myself in this new environment.

"My parents were devout Christians, and avid churchgoers who belonged to the Church of Jesus Christ and Latter Days Saints which is headquartered in Salt Lake City.

"I eventually met a boy and fell in love with him. My self-esteem was at a low point in my life. Finally, someone was showing interest in me, and I was smitten. Due to my strong religious beliefs, I felt compelled to make a commitment to marriage before giving myself to him in a physical way. That idea was also supported by my church teachings and by my parents.

"So, I was married at the age of eighteen. My new husband was 21. We immediately moved into an apartment in the local area not far from my parents. He worked as a mechanic, and I secured two jobs to make ends meet.

"Within a few months of my marriage, I began to notice that my husband was drinking more and became abusive toward me. I was a young, naive woman and wanted to please. I had no basis for comparison, as this man was my first love. His behavior escalated, and I found out later on that he was consuming illegal drugs and selling them as well to support his own habit.

"It wasn't uncommon for him to come home in the wee hours of the morning and pass out, leaving me alone and actually quite scared and confused as to what was happening. I didn't seek the counsel of anyone initially—I honestly thought that I could reason with my husband and try to understand his behavior.

"Over time, I became very upset and depressed. I had no idea why this was happening to me. Throughout this ordeal, I had been taking various medicines for severe premenstrual symptoms—bloating, cramping, aches, pains, etc. So I had available an array of drugs which my husband was taking and selling to make money to buy other drugs.

"I couldn't believe what was happening. My view of 'happily ever after' was being shattered before my eyes. Finally, I turned to my church bishop for advice. He told me try to work things out, and to seek counseling for both of us. My husband refused to go. Now here I was, all alone, with a partner I felt was dragging me down, and in my mind's eye I had no way out. I felt trapped in this situation; divorce was not an acceptable option in our religion or in my family. The situation got worse. My husband hurt me.

"The pain became too much to bear. Again, I saw no way out because of my programming and my insecurities. The situation was escalating, and my physical ailments were all crashing down on me.

"One night, when I was home alone, I decided that this was all I could take. I didn't want to wake to another day of pain and abuse thinking this was going to be my entire life. I went into the bathroom, took every pill bottle out of the medicine cabinet, and emptied them into a bowl. I started to take handfuls of these pills, and washed them down my throat. (I was later told that I took a total of 72 pills.)

"I got into bed and started to drift off. Shortly after that, I heard my husband come through the door, look in the medicine cabinet, and then storm into the bedroom. He knew at that moment that I had taken everything, and he screamed for me to get out of bed.

"At that point, I could hear him, but I was paralyzed. I couldn't even open my eyes. I could hear him call his stepfather, who was a toxicologist, for emergency advice. My husband read label after label to him, and within a minute, his stepfather advised him to call 911.

"The next thing I can remember was a room full of men attempting to stick needles in my arms. I was loaded on a stretcher and taken to a local hospital by ambulance.

"I was slipping in and out of consciousness. When they parked my stretcher in the ER, I could feel the staff cranking the bed to put me in an elevated position. I felt myself falling off the bed, and in my mind I tried to physically pull myself up. That's when the inexplicable happened.

"I was now outside of my body looking at myself, and then I started to rise above my body, like floating out and away from this entire scene towards the darkness.

"I felt free even though it was dark; I was not afraid, and there was no pain. I was lighter than a feather and felt essentially weightless. I was drawn to a light, and I crossed a threshold.

When that happened, I knew I was in God's presence, and I felt complete and utter peace. I saw my entire life flash before me. Like a movie on fast-forward, I saw everything—the good, the bad, joyful times, sorrow, all the events of my life. The movie stopped on a real scene, and I saw the face of my brother looking at me with tears in his eyes.

"I was in a place now where I was communicating telepathically with God. God told me, 'You did it. Is this what you really want? You have not fulfilled your purpose yet. Are you going to quit? You are going to have to complete your purpose, now or later. Do you want or go back and finish now, or take a harder route later?'

"I was torn. Here I was in complete and unconditional love in a place that no human words can describe. The words 'utter bliss' and 'sublime' don't even come close to what I felt.

"My brother's face stuck in my mind. I knew he was the immediate purpose, but really didn't know why. I just knew that he needed me, and that my leaving now would devastate him, and my purpose would not be fulfilled.

'I told God, "I don't think I am strong enough to face the earthly world...It's too hard.'

"God told me, 'I will always be with you to help you, and will never give you more than you can handle.'

"I laughed, and I actually joked with God and said, 'I really didn't want to leave this earthly life until I learned to play tennis properly.' I felt God's warmth and unconditional love and acceptance and glory all together simultaneously.

"I can't truly explain it, but it's like God let me go at that point, and I fell back to earth. Like the re-entry of a space capsule into the atmosphere.

"The next thing I remember, I was thrashing about and vomiting in the ER. I felt like I had been thrown against a brick wall as the weight and heavy feeling of being in a physical body came back unexpectedly.

"Then I slowly recovered physically. I conceived my son Andrew on Christmas Day that year, and I left my husband on my son's first birthday.

"My life has not been a bowl of cherries. In actuality it got worse after that experience. I married again—out of fear—another alcoholic—and because I got early signs of cancer. But through it all, I knew that God was with me always. And still is. I am not afraid of ANYTHING. I know that whatever happens in my life, that it wouldn't matter. This is ALL just temporary."

CONCLUSION

Faith and Belief

"Faith is to believe what you do not see;
the reward of this faith is to see what you believe."
Saint Augustine

Trusting and knowing that you are in God's hands and being watched all the time is the basis of hope and peace.

Three years ago, I was standing in a line at the Philadelphia airport. I started a conversation with a "seasoned" flight attendant. Somehow the subject of my illness came up. In a moment I will NEVER forget, she stared right into my eyes and said: "Why are you fooling around here? Go to Germany...they have amazing doctors. I was sick for a month and no one here could tell me what was wrong, I went there and in 30 days I was cured."

Six months ago, I went to see the renowned Lyme disease authority, Dr. Richard Horowitz in New York. He looked over my chart, and within 15 minutes of our meeting, he turned to me and asked: "You have failed many treatments and seen many good physicians. Have you considered Germany? It is an option in your treatment protocol."

In fact, I took Dr. Horowitz's advice and recently went to Germany, and received "cutting-edge" treatments not available in the United States. The town I went to, by the way, has St. George as its patron. My final treatment was on St. George's Day on the Christian calendar. I am doing better today and believe I will be completely well!

I embrace the quote: "God does not expect the impossible from us...He wants us to expect the impossible from him."

In the Book of Mark there is a poignant story about faith and prayer that exemplifies the power of belief.

The disciples attempted but failed to heal an epileptic boy. His frantic father was seeking their help when Jesus came on the scene. Jesus understood immediately what was happening and why they had been unable to heal the boy.

The father asked Jesus for help, and Jesus explained that he could help but only if they the father had faith. With faith and prayer would come a cure.

From the Holy Bible, Mark 9, 21-24

21 Jesus asked the boy's father, "How long has he been like this?"

"Since he was a child," he answered. 22 "The spirit has often thrown him into fire or water to kill him. But if you can do anything, take pity on us. Please help us."

23 " 'If you can'?" said Jesus. "Everything is possible for the one who believes."

24 Right away the boy's father cried out, "I do believe! Help me overcome my unbelief!"

Jesus explained that there would be times when we're faced with seemingly insurmountable obstacles, but with belief and prayer, miracles can happen. Because the disciples and the father had doubt, the healing was not occurring. But with faith, it could happen. Jesus stood over the boy and commanded him to be healed and he was.

The story helps us to see that if we fail to pray, we fail. But with belief and faith, all things including miracles are possible.

I know how difficult it can be to "just believe" at times. When the world I had known was collapsing, nothing that was said made a difference. I had attended church all my life, performed acts of kindness, and had always been a "good guy." None of that mattered when I lost hope. It took that one encounter with Maureen Hancock to "awaken" me and allow me to have hope, and then open my heart and mind to truly believe. Have you had such a moment?

Reaching higher and KNOWING (believing) that you are in God's plan is the key.

Information on Lyme Disease

The exhaustive three and a half year battle I describe to correctly diagnose and finally cure my Lyme disease, may seem like a rare story - a medical oddity. In fact, my story is not nearly as unusual as you might think.

Especially in the US where lab tests for Lyme are not as good as they could be, the lab work for the disease frequently comes back indicating a false positive.

The CDC recently released a report indicating that Lyme Disease is about then times more common than previously reported Health officials say as many as 300,000 Americans are actually diagnosed with Lyme Disease each year. Previously, the CDC had said that number ranged from 20,000 to 30,000. Health officials said doctors don't always report every case, and the true count was much higher.

A July 8, 2013 article from the *New York Times' Well* blog (*When Lyme Disease Lasts and Lasts*) points out how frequently the illness is misdiagnosed, mistreated and that every year, says the *Times'* blog, thousands of people are left "mentally debilitated and without a medically established recourse."

How widespread the disease has become is further suggested by the comments I received following a mention of my struggles on another site's blog. Here are a random few of them:

KDK -"I have a friend who went undiagnosed for 9 or more years. She kept saying that she had Lyme, and the doctors kept saying no. She finally got the diagnosis and correct treatment. Her levels were so high they said she shouldn't be walking AT ALL. She is now crippled with arthritis and a multitude of other ailments."

***

SDF - "My daughter Isabella has been ill since January with it."

***

NK - "I was only properly diagnosed because I had a co-infection."

***

CL - "My fiancé had Lyme disease and the first treatment didn't work so they had to put a stint in this chest for a month, scary stuff.

***

CP - "OMG, My husband has been fighting that very same thing for the past 12 years. The tests are negative except for one and still the doctors say he doesn't have it. It has ruined our lives and hope.

***

CSL - My close friend's teenage daughter has been seriously struggling for 3 yrs. My friend has done a lot of research and even has to deal with doctors that say their daughter is crazy - just what a teenager doesn't need to hear. As well as struggles with their health insurance. So much for this poor girl's teenage years.

***

LFW - Yup. I had it too, in 1998. Misdiagnosed for 5 months. SO glad it didn't become chronic but still have residual joint pains.

***

SH - "In most cases it just needs to be a simple test...and if you don't get a correct reading...ask/demand again."

LYME DISEASE RESOURCES

Lyme Disease is complex. You may not know that you have Lyme. It can mimic many disease processes including Chronic Fatigue Syndrome, Fibromyalgia, autoimmune conditions like MS, psychiatric conditions like depression and anxiety, and it can cause significant memory and concentration problems, mimicking early dementia. It is called the "Great Imitator," and inaccurate testing—combined with a fierce, ongoing debate that questions chronic infection—make it difficult for sufferers to get a proper diagnosis or to find effective care.

Not only is the Lyne Disease difficult to test for and deal with, but more and more pathogens are being discovered, carried by ticks, that mimic Lyme Disease symptoms, yet tests for them are not widely available.

Two newly discovered ones, as noted in a *New York Times* August 12, 2013 article, are the Borrelia miyamotoi, which is best described as disease with many Lyme-like symptoms: fatigue, muscle and joint pain, headaches and serious neurological symptoms. But the problem is, the *Times* article points out, that there is no widely available blood test for this pathogen.

A second newly discovered pathogen, Powassan encephalitis, is transmitted within minutes, notes Dr. Richard I. Horowitz, in his book, *"Why Can't I Get Better?: Solving the Mystery of Lyme and Chronic Disease."* This one is deadly 30% of the time, and it's transmitted by the same ticks that carry Lyme Disease.

What is worse, many doctors are unfamiliar with the constellations of symptoms and long lasting effects of this debilitating disease. It took me YEARS and hundreds of thousand of dollars to find the right doctors with the courage and compassion to treat me and, ultimately, save my life. There are many well meaning, bright doctors. Most are not Lyme literate.

Don't waste your time with physicians who tell you that: "We can't find anything," or "It's all in your head." Don't walk, run out of those medical offices. You know your body and don't ever let anyone tell you that you're not experiencing symptoms. I have spoken and met with individuals who have lost their homes, marriages, life savings and careers as a result of this elusive disease.

If nothing becomes apparent from initial office visits, then demand a Lyme disease test. I have spoken with scores of doctors who privately admitted that they are shocked at the growing number of patients who are testing positive.

Dr. Richard Horowitz is clearly one of this country's foremost doctors when it comes to diagnosing, treating and healing Lyme, and peeling away the layers that lead to chronic disease. He and his team are an excellent resource and they personally treat me. Dr. Horowitz is brilliant and seasoned. I appreciate his aggressive integrative approach.

When Dr. Richard Horowitz moved to Hudson Valley, New York over two decades ago to start his own medical practice, he had no idea that he was jumping into a hotbed of Lyme disease. He would soon realize that many of the chronic disease diagnoses people were receiving were also the result of Lyme—and he would discover how once-treatable infections, in the absence of timely intervention, could cause disabling conditions. In a field where the number of cases is growing exponentially around the world and answers remain elusive, Dr. Horowitz has treated over 12,000 patients and made extraordinary progress. His plan represents a crucial paradigm shift, without which the suffering will continue.

Dr. Horowitz's book should be read by everyone. Among other things, it covers in detail Lyme's leading symptoms and co-infections, including immune dysfunction, sleep disorders, chronic pain and neurodegenerative disorders—providing a unique functional and integrative health care model, based on the most up-to-date scientific research, for physicians and health care providers to effectively treat Lyme and other chronic illnesses.

For other medical providers and Lyme disease resources, contact me on my website: www.AngelsWalkingWithUs.net

ABOUT THE AUTHOR

George Popovici is an award winning, certified safety engineer. He holds a degree in Industrial Technology and has sat on several national level technical committees and authored articles on incident prevention.

George now devotes much of his time to helping others who are ill through his charity. He also speaks to groups and organizations. George lives in New England with his children. Contact George at: www.AngelsWalkingWithUs.net